SINGLE ASIAN FEMALE

Michelle Law

Currency Press,
Sydney

CURRENCY PLAYS

First published in 2018
by Currency Press Pty Ltd,
Gadigal Land, Suite 310, 46–56 Kippax Street, Surry Hills, NSW 2010, Australia
enquiries@currency.com.au
www.currency.com.au

in association with Belvoir, Sydney.

Reprinted 2022, 2024.

Typeset by Dean Nottle for Currency Press.
Printed by CanPrint, Canberra.
Cover design: Alphabet Studio.

Currency Press acknowledges the Traditional Owners of the Country on which we live and work. We pay our respects to all Aboriginal and Torres Strait Islander Elders, past and present.

A catalogue record for this book is available from the National Library of Australia

Contents

Single Asian Female was first produced by La Boite Theatre Company at the Roundhouse Theatre, Brisbane, on 11 February 2017, with the following cast:

KATIE	Emily Burton
PAUL	Patrick Jhanur
ZOE	Alex Lee
MEI	Courtney Stewart
PEARL	Hsiao-Ling Tang
LANA	Emily Vascotto

Director, Claire Christian
Set and Costume Designer, Moe Assaad
Lighting Designer, Keith Clark
Sound Designer and Composer, Wil Hughes
Fight Director, N-J Price
Stage Manager, Peter Sutherland
Assistant Stage Manager, Katie Hurst

Belvoir subsequently presented the La Boite Theatre Company production at Belvoir St Theatre, opening on 17 February 2018, with Lucy Heffernan playing the role of Lana and Keiren Smith as Assistant Stage Manager.

CHARACTERS

PEARL, 50s. A Chinese migrant who moved from Hong Kong to Australia 30 years ago. She's an overprotective and proudly traditional Chinese mother, however she's quite progressive in other ways—she's a feminist, foul-mouthed and runs her own business. She recently divorced her abusive husband, a decision that drove a wedge between her and her daughters. Pearl is desperate to preserve her relationships with her westernised children; when it comes to them she's grappling with generational as well as cultural barriers.

ZOE, 29. An A-type musician experiencing a quarter-life crisis. Zoe is desperate to secure a job in an orchestra so that she can gain independence from her smothering mother (Pearl), who is pressuring her to settle down, and be a good role model for her younger sister (Mei). She has chronic anxiety and is prone to panic attacks. Zoe is the golden child who extinguishes fires within the family and has always been Pearl's right-hand woman. She has an awkward relationship with Mei and struggles to connect with her.

MEI, 17. A self-hating Asian who's desperate to fit in with her Anglo peers. She's embarrassed by her Chinese family, especially her mother Pearl. Mei lashes out to conceal her vulnerability; deep down, she is more like the dutiful and loving Asian daughter stereotype that she's trying so hard to reject. Reading is her passion and she uses it as a way to escape drama at home. She resents Zoe and Pearl's closeness and misses her father. Mei feels like she doesn't quite belong anywhere, both at home and at school.

PAUL, 30s. Zoe's love interest and Pearl's lawyer. Paul was a refugee; he and his family sought asylum in Australia when he was a child. He works immigration cases at Legal Aid, fighting for those people he recognised needed help when he was growing up. He's self-deprecating and awkward in a very charming way. And he's caring enough to handle Zoe's anxiety.

KATIE, 17. Mei's best friend. Katie is a bit of a social outcast, but she doesn't let it get to her; she's proud of who she is and her nerdy love of cosplay and manga. Katie loves Asian culture and Mei's family, and is earnest in a way that makes her unintentionally funny. She recognises that Mei is going through an identity crisis but doesn't want to interfere.

LANA, 17. Mei's frenemy. Lana bullies Mei and Katie in both overt and underhanded ways to distract herself from her fractured home life; she wants to regain some semblance of control. Lana takes joy in belittling Mei because her own father is engaged to a young Asian woman of whom Lana is jealous.

CLAUDIA, a violinist.

SETTING

A dated, family-run Chinese restaurant on the Sunshine Coast, Queensland.

An interval can be taken in Act Two between Scenes Three and Four.

PROLOGUE

SCENE ONE

Evening in a dinky Chinese restaurant decorated with paper lanterns and fairy lights. PEARL *stands on a small stage as the instrumentals for 'I Will Survive' by Gloria Gaynor plays.* PEARL *sings the first verse.*

PEARL: This is one of my favourite songs, and I sing it to you tonight in celebration of my divorce being officially finalised! I left my dickhead husband years ago, but at last Pearl is a free woman: a reborn virgin. And if you only count good sex, the kind that finishes with the capital 'O' Orgasm, then technically I have been a virgin for most of my life with this man. But now! Now, I am an oyster. No. What is the saying? Ah! The world is my oyster. It may surprise you to know that it was never Pearl's dream to run a restaurant, although I do it very well. Many people assume that all Chinese people love to cook, that it runs in their blood, that it's their passion in life. *So stupid.* When we leave our home countries we open restaurants because what else can we do? We are second-class citizens. Third-class citizens. When my father was a young man he migrated from China to Malaysia and opened a restaurant in Ipoh. 'If you start a business, make it a restaurant,' he used to say. 'Why? Because we all share hunger in common.' Even if you are the dirt under a shoe and people call you 'Ching Chong' and do the slit-eye thing, they will still smile, eat your food, yummy yummy, get fat, hopefully have a heart attack sooner than later. They go to Bali for their holidays to buy cheap clothes and drink too much and have sex with young girls and boys. And then they come back with a Buddha statue, plop it on their lawn and vote for Pauline Hanson.

Pause.

Uh … but I'm not talking about you, my loyal customers! Seeing your beautiful faces each week is a joy to Pearl and please don't forget that the special tonight is free corkage with any serving of vegetarian spring rolls.

Pause.

I am sick of this place. Everything in this place smells like oil. It gets into your skin. I've been a slave in this restaurant for most of my life. How funny, right? You move somewhere for a better life and instead you find yourself thinking every day, 'I wonder if things would have turned out better if I'd stayed put. I wonder what would have happened if I married my ex-boyfriend instead of this man.' Every day: 'Pearl! Cut this beef!' On my birthday: 'Pearl! Peel these carrots!' On our anniversary: 'Pearl! Wash my clothes!' On Chinese New Year: 'Feed the babies, I'm going to mah jong with my buddies.' Hello? Am I a fucking robot? Excuse my language. But where is Pearl's relaxation? Where are Pearl's buddies? Oh yeah, I forgot: Pearl has no friends. I can never go to see a movie. I can never wear nice things like this *cheongsam*. This is a dress my mother bought for me before I left Hong Kong. 'You're married now. You have to follow your husband,' she said.

Pause.

I could have been a CEO. I could have a degree. Pearl, with a doctorate. [*Giggling*] Why am I laughing? I like the sound of Doctor Pearl. I could have married someone good—no! I could have stayed single. All of the women here should know that in this modern age, the world is your oyster. And you definitely do not need a man in that oyster. There is such thing as a vibrator.

The backing track to 'I Will Survive' starts up again.

Now, you can clap along if you like. But not too loudly because you still want to hear my beautiful voice, of course.

[*Singing*] And so you're back
From Hong Kong
I just walked in to find
That you were seeing call girls all along
I should have changed that stupid lock
I should have kicked you on the streets
If I had known for just one second
You'd try to screw up my life

Go on now go
Walk out the door
Just turn around now
I'll run the restaurant all alone
Weren't you the one who tried to hurt me—

She speaks above the music.

First with the cheating—all the overnight 'business' meetings, then the gambling, then the abuse, physical and emotional, but emotional still counts, it still leaves a big scar. Oh, sorry—

The music plays on and PEARL *sings the chorus.*

The word 'SINGLE.' flashes above PEARL *in neon lights, much like the 'OPEN' sign you might see at a Chinese restaurant.*

SCENE TWO

Afternoon in Mei's bedroom. MEI *moves around the room in damp swimmers, shoving any identifiably 'Asian' objects into a garbage bag. Her best friend* KATIE *watches on helplessly.*

MEI: And then she just casually kept playing volleyball as if nothing had happened, like I'd just imagined it.

KATIE: She could have been talking to someone else. There were heaps of people on the beach.

MEI: Katie! She wasn't. Can't you just trust me on this?

KATIE: You know Lana has weird anger issues. The other day, Kelsey said she was getting the same colour formal dress as Lana and Lana literally kicked her in the vagina. She had to get stitches. And just because Kelsey was getting the same colour dress! Not even the same style. So, you know, Lana could have easily been going off at someone else and you were just standing in the firing range.

MEI: She called me a gook.

KATIE: Oh.

MEI: And a fob.

KATIE: What's a fob?

MEI: Someone who's 'fresh off the boat'. [*Shoving a soft toy into the garbage bag*] *This* has got to go.

KATIE: Mei, you're getting rid of Rilakkuma? I got him for your birthday.

MEI: Sorry. It's just part of the purge. Look at all the Asian stuff in this room! Lana was right: I didn't even realise how much of a fob I was.

KATIE: You're not a fob! You were born in Nambour. That's the most Aussie you can get. Kevin Rudd was born there and look what happened to him!

MEI: He learnt how to speak Mandarin?

KATIE: No, that's a bad example.

MEI: I didn't realise until today that there are no other Asians at school.

KATIE: What about Christopher?

MEI: I mean Asians that I'm not related to in some way. And no-one ever pays Christopher out because he's basically white anyway. Remember on his first day he couldn't even talk properly because he'd lived in Hong Kong his whole life. 'Hurro, hurro.' He just followed me around every day and sat next to me in class because he needed me to translate everything the teacher said. Now he ignores me and just hangs out with the rugby crew.

KATIE: What makes you a fob and Christopher not, though? I don't see the difference between him and you.

MEI: Racist much.

KATIE: I didn't mean it that way!

MEI: Well … I eat Chinese food for lunch every day. No-one else at school does that. Everything I own smells like mothballs. I play the violin. I'm so short-sighted I'm basically blind. And my nose can't even hold my glasses up properly. My name literally means 'Rice' in Cantonese!

KATIE: I'd love to eat Chinese food for lunch every day.

MEI: I don't know why you're so obsessed with Asian culture, Katie. You should be happy you're white. [*Pulling clothes from the wardrobe and tossing them on the bed*] Blouse for Chinese school. String ensemble trousers. Jelly shoes. Doraemon face mask. Hello Kitty pyjamas. Puffy vest. I just want to start over.

KATIE: Hey, these shoes are really cute. Such a great colour! You should wear them to the formal. And so comfortable! [*Removing the shoes*] Oh, sorry! No shoes inside. I always forget.

MEI: Can you imagine what I've stepped in, wearing those shoes? I wore them in Hong Kong at the Ladies' Market and in squat toilets. There could even be poo on them! Sorry, I'm overreacting. It's fine.

KATIE: It's my fault.

MEI: No, it's fine! You can even wear them on the bed if you want. That's what you'd do at home, right?

KATIE: I guess so … I haven't really thought about it. Are you sure it's okay? [*Off* MEI*'s look*] I'm taking them off. I'm stretching them, anyway.

MEI: You can have them if you want.

KATIE: Really?

MEI: You can have any of this stuff.

KATIE: Can I have the vest?

MEI: [*nuzzling against the vest*] Ooh, so soft. No! Just take it. Whatever you don't take I'm going to donate anyway.

KATIE: But this is like, all of your clothes.

MEI: I'll buy new clothes. I've been saving the pocket money my dad gives me.

KATIE: We could go op-shopping. Oh! What if you found your formal dress there? It'd be one of a kind. Can you imagine what people would say?

MEI: Probably nothing good. I've already picked a dress, anyway…

KATIE: Really! Can I see?

MEI: [*furtively*] It's at my dad's and I don't want to bother him.

MEI *removes her glasses and moves her arms around blindly.*

KATIE: What are you doing?

MEI: I want to try something. Pick something up and throw it at me.

KATIE: What?

MEI: I want to see if I can get around without my glasses. Contacts make my eyes really itchy. Are you throwing anything yet?

A book hits MEI *in the face.*

Ow. Not a book, Katie! Jesus.

The word 'ASIAN.' flashes above MEI *in neon lights.*

SCENE THREE

Afternoon in an audition waiting room. ZOE *sits with her violin case in her lap. She wears a baggy men's shirt and pores over sheet music. Another woman,* CLAUDIA, *tunes her violin nearby, watching* ZOE *intently.* ZOE *receives a text message and giggles at it before typing out a response.*

CLAUDIA: [*whispering*] Zoe? Hey, Zoe.
ZOE: Hi, Claudia.

ZOE *smiles politely and goes back to texting.*

CLAUDIA: Phones need to be on silent.
ZOE: Right! Sorry. [*Putting her phone away*] How are you feeling?
CLAUDIA: Good! But I wore my lucky socks just in case. I know it's silly.
ZOE: I eat a chocolate muffin before every audition.
CLAUDIA: [*surveying Zoe's outfit*] Did you get much rehearsal in yesterday?
ZOE: Just in the afternoon. I don't want it to sound overcooked.
CLAUDIA: Oh, there's no way it could! You're too talented. Jeremy and I were just saying that you played so gorgeously at our wedding. His brother Lucas was asking about you afterwards.
ZOE: Was he the one who lives in Beijing?
CLAUDIA: Lucas is one of the last good guys out there. Honestly, I fear for any woman still braving the dating scene. You should let me know when you're free—I'll set you guys up.
ZOE: That's really sweet of you … but I'll have to check my diary first. Sorry, I don't mean to be rude, but …

ZOE *points at her sheet music.*

CLAUDIA: Absolutely! I'll shut up, let you get in the zone.

After a beat, CLAUDIA *starts sniffing the air.*

Is that … are you wearing cologne? It smells like Intimately Yours by David Beckham.
ZOE: [*distracted*] What?
CLAUDIA: Who is he?
ZOE: Who's who?
CLAUDIA: Don't play dumb. You had sex last night!
ZOE: That's none of your business.
CLAUDIA: Oh, my goodness. Is it Kyle from percussion? He's liked you for ages.
ZOE: [*hissing*] Can we talk about this later? Away from here? [*Sniffing herself*] And it's Tom Ford, not David Beckham.
CLAUDIA: Zoe Wong, you snake in the grass! I thought you were single!
ZOE: I am. I just met this guy online and we hung out last night.
CLAUDIA: You mean, like … from Tinder?

ZOE: We had drinks and I didn't have time to go back to my apartment to change, so …

CLAUDIA: Oh.

ZOE: Lucky my violin was in the car.

Pause.

I don't do this all the time. Not that there's anything wrong with that. Women are free to do whatever they want with their bodies with whoever they want.

CLAUDIA: Zoe, don't worry. Your secret's safe with me. Did you use protection though?

ZOE: [*hissing*] Claudia.

CLAUDIA: Chlamydia rates are rising! You don't know where people have been.

ZOE: [*bluntly*] Or where I've been?

CLAUDIA: Zoe, I'm just trying to look out for you. Woman to woman.

ZOE: Yes, we used a condom. There was an accident, but I'm on the pill so it's fine.

CLAUDIA: An accident?

ZOE: The condom broke, but—

CLAUDIA: What do you mean, 'broke'? Like, it tore or overflowed?

ZOE: Overflowed? Christ. Does it matter?

CLAUDIA: Once Jeremy's condom broke before I made him get screened. Lucky he was wearing two of them.

ZOE: Look, we were both consenting adults who— Wait. What?

CLAUDIA: And you're worth so much more than hooking up with strangers! Don't you think we're at a life stage where that's just a bit … you know?

ZOE: A bit what?

ZOE *and* CLAUDIA *eye each other until* CLAUDIA *is summoned into the audition room.*

CLAUDIA: Oh! Break a leg.

ZOE *smiles at* CLAUDIA *as she exits.*

ZOE: [*sweetly*] I'll break your neck.

She removes her violin from its case and angrily resins the bow. After a beat her phone rings.

[*On her phone*] Mum, I'm at the audition. Yep, any second now so can I call you back?

Pause.

Mum, slow down. No, I don't have time to do that. Let's talk about it later.

A beat.

Are you kidding me? Fuck! Well, where am I supposed to live?

The word 'FEMALE.' flashes above her in neon lights.

END OF PROLOGUE

ACT ONE

Daytime in Mei's room. Zoe's luggage has been dumped haphazardly around the place; her suitcase is open on Mei's bed. ZOE *wears faded, old clothes—she's been moving house all day.* MEI, *now wearing contact lenses and a slick hairdo, kicks Zoe's suitcase off the bed.*

ZOE: Mei!

MEI: It was an accident!

ZOE: Now I have to fold everything up again.

MEI: It must be annoying to have all your things out of place.

ZOE: Enough with the attitude.

MEI: How long are you staying for?

ZOE: You think I want to be here? Stuck in my old room and—

MEI: It's *my* room. It has been for ages.

> MEI *picks a book up and starts reading.* ZOE *folds her clothes. A long silence.* ZOE *brings her clothes to the wardrobe and pulls out an old Missy Higgins T-shirt.*

ZOE: I used to wear this shirt all the time. Mum hated it. She said it was too tight-fit.

MEI: I never wear it. I don't even know who that is.

ZOE: Mei, its Missy Higgins.

MEI: Plus, it's huge on me. All your hand-me-downs are like tents.

> ZOE *waves the shirt around and sings the first line of the chorus of Missy Higgins' 'Scar'.*

ZOE: Maybe they've just stretched over time.

MEI: They haven't. Anyway, it's fine. I mostly swap clothes with my friends.

ZOE: Which friends?

MEI: You don't know them.

ZOE: Are you and Katie still friends?

MEI: Yeah, of course.

ZOE: Who else is there?

MEI: Lots of other people. Jess, Yolanda, Nikki, Reese, Lana—

ZOE: Lana Paton? Bart Paton's younger sister? Didn't their dad have an affair with his Asian assistant or something?

MEI: Yeah, then their mum had nervous breakdown and moved to New Zealand.

ZOE: God.

Pause.

At camp one year, Bart shoved a goldfish in an empty Coke bottle and threw it against a brick wall until the fish died. He got expelled.

MEI: Yeah, but he sounds like a psycho. Lana can be nice—

ZOE: When she wants to be?

MEI *ignores* ZOE *and types on her phone.* ZOE *stares at the phone wide-eyed.*

When did you get a new phone?

MEI: Ages ago.

ZOE: Dad's giving you way too much pocket money.

MEI: I wouldn't have needed to buy one if your hand-me-down didn't break.

ZOE: [*ignoring her*] Where's Mum?

MEI: Uni. Getting a student card.

ZOE: Hah. So she's actually still enrolled. Good for her.

Pause.

That sounded really sarcastic, but I actually am happy for her.

ZOE *receives a text message. She giggles to herself and types out a response. Then she clocks her scattered belongings as if for the first time and panic sets in. She starts pacing, on the verge of a panic attack.* MEI *watches* ZOE, *uninterested, and continues reading.*

What's *Jane Eyre* about?

MEI: It's just a book I'm reading for school.

ZOE: Right. What's the story?

MEI: A lot happens, but it's about this girl who grows up basically alone and she feels totally isolated … but then she rises above it all and finds love and family after never wavering from her principles. People always say it's a romance novel but it's really about her evolution as a person.

ZOE: Wow. I didn't know you were so into literature.

MEI: That's what I said in my English oral, anyway.

She keeps reading, embarrassed at having given away too much. ZOE *deep breathes and plays classical music on her phone. She pulls an air mattress from the wardrobe.*

Can you turn it down a bit?

ZOE *does.*

Zoe …

ZOE *turns it down more.*

It's still a bit—

ZOE *turns the music off.*

ZOE: I'm pissed too, Mei. This is only temporary while I convince Mum not to sell my apartment—

MEI: It's not *your* apartment—

ZOE: So can you just stop acting like a spoilt brat for one second? At least you don't have to sleep on a bloody air mattress.

Pause.

Where's my pillow? I thought I put it on top of my clothes … where the hell is it?!

MEI: I wasn't angry and I wasn't being a brat! The music was just a bit loud and I couldn't concentrate. You're the one who's in a bad mood so don't take it out on me.

MEI *rubs her eyes.*

ZOE: Are you crying?

MEI: No! My contact lenses are itchy.

ZOE *receives a text message. She texts back excitedly while taking deep breaths.* MEI *watches her and wordlessly offers a bottle of water. A beat as* ZOE *drinks and reads her phone.*

ZOE: You know, I was thinking. There's a good chance you'll make it into the Conservatory if you nail the piece we've been working on. I think you're close. I got in on the same audition piece and if you mention to them that I'm your sister, not in an obvious way, they'll probably—

MEI: I quit the ensemble.

ZOE: What?

MEI: A couple of weeks ago now. It isn't fun anymore.

ZOE: Mei! You should have said something.

MEI: You and Mum would have gotten angry. You had to make the trip here every weekend—

ZOE: I wouldn't have gotten angry. I only pushed you so hard because you had talent and I thought you enjoyed it.

MEI: Are you mad?

ZOE: No, I'm not mad. But you would have saved us both a lot of trouble if you'd said something earlier. And petrol! It's expensive driving back and forth between here and Brisbane.

MEI: Mum doesn't know, so don't say anything because she's already crazy enough about controlling everything as it is.

ZOE: She's going to find out eventually.

MEI: Yeah, but can you just not say anything right now?

ZOE: I'm telling you, Mei, she's going to find out somehow.

MEI: You always do this. When are you going? I'm sleeping in the laundry until then.

ZOE: Mei, that's silly.

MEI: There isn't enough space up here for both of us.

ZOE: Don't be such a child.

MEI: I need my pillow.

ZOE: If you're going to act like this, I'll go. I'll take the air mattress downstairs.

> MEI *goes to exit and* ZOE *follows her. They run into* PEARL *at the door.* PEARL *holds bags of groceries and wears a wide-brimmed cap.*

PEARL: [*to* MEI] What are you doing?

ZOE: [*to* PEARL] What are you wearing?

MEI: I'm not sharing a room with Zoe.

ZOE: Mum, I need somewhere to put my bags.

PEARL: There's enough space in your room.

MEI: It's *my* room!

PEARL: It's both of your rooms, lah. Both of my babies. Mei, put down those sheets—they're dragging on the floor, collecting all the dust. So dirty.

ZOE: This isn't going to work, Mum.

MEI: Did you pick up my parcel? It's my formal shoes.

PEARL: Oh, no. I've been at the university all day returning textbooks.

ZOE: You don't have to say, 'At the university'. Just say, 'At uni'. No-one calls it university.

PEARL: Excuse me, Little Miss Snobby. I speak three languages. How many can you speak? Just one.

MEI: Didn't you buy those books yesterday? Are they damaged?

PEARL: I decided I'm too busy for university right now. Running the restaurant is a big job for one person. I have to focus on the renovations now.

ZOE: What renovations?

PEARL: Ah. [*Caught out*] We're giving the restaurant a new look, from top to bottom. So we have to clear everything out. I've already put the new hours up: from now on we only open on Friday for dinner.

ZOE: What about lunch hours?

PEARL: No more lunch until everything is sorted.

ZOE: Mum, you can't afford to do that.

Pause.

Is this why you sold my apartment?

MEI: It's not your apartment!

PEARL: No. The Brisbane apartment was tied up with other things.

ZOE: Is it because you couldn't handle uni? If you want help understanding assignments—

PEARL: Zozo, please shut the eff up. Mummy is very smart. Smarter than most people. University isn't going anywhere. Right now I have the restaurant to take care of, and the rest of the apartment sale, the community work, and meeting with all those people—

ZOE: What people?

PEARL: Ai ya, my plate is already full up with all this shits!

ZOE: Mum, I wasn't saying you weren't smart enough.

Beat.

So you've already quit?

PEARL: Please, change the subject. Mummy is tired from running around all day like her head chop off.

MEI: Mum, remember I have friends coming over for dinner tomorrow night.

PEARL: Okay. Katie is coming over. That's fine.

MEI: Mum! It was a big table of us. I told you last week.

PEARL: How many people in total?

MEI: Seven. I told them they don't have to pay.

PEARL: Why did you tell them that? Seven is a lot of people. They must pay.

MEI: But I told them it would be free.

PEARL: Nothing in life is free. Fifty per cent discount. That's my final offer. It will be good lesson for those Aussie kids that you must work very hard in life.

MEI: [*muttering*] Dad never made my friends pay …

PEARL: *Lei gong mi?* [What did you say?]

MEI: Nothing.

ZOE: Are you going to buy a new apartment once you finish the renovations?

PEARL: I don't think so.

ZOE: Mum! I can't keep my stuff in storage forever.

PEARL: I already apologised, Zozo.

ZOE: No, you didn't! Do you know how difficult it was to get all of my shit—?

PEARL: Language.

ZOE: All of my *stuff* together? I had back-to-back auditions the whole week and then at night I had to pack, and then I'd be up at five the next day for work and my skin is breaking out and my back won't stop aching … I can't stay here.

She starts hyperventilating.

PEARL: You're tired from the drive. What did you have for lunch?

ZOE: I didn't have lunch.

PEARL: I'll make you some noodles. Do you want something to drink?

ZOE: I'm fine.

PEARL: How about a soft drink? Coke? Sprite? Pasito?

ZOE: Maybe I'll have a Pasito.

MEI: You never let me have soft drinks!

PEARL: Ai ya, it's a special occasion. How often does your sister come home to stay with us? Once in a blue moon.

MEI *barges past* PEARL *and* ZOE, *carrying her bedding.* PEARL *hurries after her.*

Mei, where are you going!

MEI *goes downstairs into the living room (which doubles as the restaurant), knocking over things as she goes. We see the restaurant properly for the first time: it's dinky, dated and carpeted, with a rose pink interior and wooden fans splayed on the walls. Downstairs, there is a bathroom, kitchen, and storage room.*

MEI: I'm sleeping in the laundry.

PEARL: Do you know how many cockroaches live there? Come here, don't be crazy.

Pause.

You should sleep in the storage room. It's much cleaner.

MEI: Piss off!

PEARL: Piss off? I'll piss off when I'm dead! Then you'll feel guilty. Then you'll know how lucky you are to have a mummy like me, how you took Mummy for granted. Think about it. You only get one mother. That's it!

MEI *enters the storage room and slams the door.* ZOE *fills a mug with water and sits down in a booth. She picks up paper napkins and starts folding them.* PEARL *hovers outside the storage room before moving to the kitchen. She pulls a vat of stir-fry from the fridge and begins angrily filling takeaway containers.*

[*To* ZOE] Hungry?

ZOE: No.

PEARL *plonks a container of food before* ZOE.

PEARL: You lost weight.

ZOE: I've been stressed. Money's tight.

PEARL: But musicians can earn a lot of money! Like that saxophone man …

ZOE: What saxophone man?

PEARL: The bald man who plays at Carols by Candlelight.

ZOE: You mean James Morrison? Firstly, he plays the trumpet. They're two different instruments.

PEARL: Whatever.

ZOE: Unless you're André Rieu you're not going to get far playing violin unless you're part of an orchestra.

PEARL: So why don't you be part of an orchestra?

ZOE: I've been trying. It feels like I've been auditioning forever.

PEARL: But it's your dream, right? What does Mummy always say? If you work hard, treat people right—

ZOE: It's not just about hard work! It's about who you know and who your parents know and whether or not you've got a dick. And if you're not white, you can just fuck off. Sorry, I know—language. Other people only have to do half as much to get twice as far. And I have to work my arse off to even be seen.

PEARL: Yeah, those people have so much prejudice.

ZOE: *Privilege*. But yeah, they also have prejudice too.

PEARL: Mummy understands. Other dickhead idiots are in charge of your life. But you have to fight! You can't wait for other people to change things for you.

ZOE: Ugh. I'm tired of fighting. And I'm gassy.

ZOE farts and PEARL waves it away.

PEARL: The silver lining is that you get to spend quality time with Mummy and Mei.

ZOE: On the Sunshine Coast! God—it hasn't changed much, has it?

PEARL: You don't feel like this is your home anymore. You made a life for yourself somewhere else.

ZOE: Exactly.

Pause.

What did you end up making for them?

PEARL: Spring rolls. Fried rice. Sweet and sour pork. Whatever makes the *gwei lo* [white people] happy. Oh, Zozo. You should have seen the organiser's reaction when I said I will cook for the food van. Because normally it's all pastries and biscuits—boring white people food! Not yummy, hot, Chinese takeaway. And all types of people come to enjoy Mummy's cooking. Old ladies who just want to talk because they're so lonely after their children left them at a nursing home to die. Or families living below the poverty line. Can you imagine? People who are so poor that they can't afford to feed their children. So moral of the story is, at the end of the day, you are a very lucky girl.

ZOE: Mm-hm.

PEARL: It's good to help others who aren't as lucky as you. It makes you feel peaceful inside, so makes your skin look very healthy.

ZOE: Since when did you even start this community work?! A week ago?

PEARL: That's not the point.

ZOE: You hate the community.

PEARL: Not hate! Hate is a very strong word. I *dislike* some people in the community. Like when I first moved to Australia I went to the Clinique counter at the chemist to ask about moisturiser and the woman said I couldn't afford it. It was just like that scene in *Pretty Woman* except I am not a prostitute.

Pause.

You shouldn't drink tea before bed. You won't be able to fall asleep.

ZOE: It's just hot water.

PEARL: Remember when you asked Poh Poh for a mug of spicy water? And she was so confused! I had to interrupt and explain that you meant 'hot' like the temperature.

ZOE: I'm still so bad at Cantonese.

PEARL: You're better than Mei. You got to spend more time with Poh Poh and your Kau Fu and Kau Mo so it rubbed off on you.

ZOE: When was the last time you spoke to them?

PEARL: [*evasively*] I might have some hot water too.

ZOE: Mum?

PEARL: I think I will go to sleep soon.

ZOE: Mum! I was asking about Kau Fu and Kau Mo.

PEARL: Which ones?

ZOE: The ones in Hong Kong!

PEARL: What about them?

ZOE: When was the last time you spoke to them?

PEARL: Oh. Not for a very long time. Maybe four years. Five. They're very busy. So am I, running a restaurant and raising children like a single mum. I saw on the Facebook that David got married.

ZOE: Oh yeah.

PEARL: His wife isn't as pretty as you.

ZOE: She's Eurasian. She's prettier than everyone.

PEARL: I don't think so! Such big teeth.

ZOE: Yeah. Huge teeth. No. I'm happy for David. They just moved to Vancouver because she's Canadian. I think. From what I've seen on Facebook.

PEARL: But he barely knows this woman! Less than a year after you broke up and suddenly he has a wife?

ZOE: It's none of my business. And men are the last thing on my mind.

PEARL: [*deadly serious*] Zozo. Are you … the lesbian? Because Mummy is okay with that. Penny Wong has children and a white wife, you know?

ZOE: No, Mum, I'm not a lesbian.

PEARL: Okay, but if you change your mind let Mummy know first.

ZOE: Why would I do that?

PEARL: What about Jonathan? I saw him recently at Woolworths. He's very handsome these days.

ZOE: Jonathan our *cousin*?

PEARL: Are you cousins?

ZOE: Mum! He's Dad's cousin's son.

PEARL: Oh my God.

ZOE: Right now I'm focusing on getting a contract so I can go full-time. All of my friends have mortgages and kids and superannuation and I'm … stuck here.

PEARL: It's good to be close to Mummy.

ZOE *receives a text message. She reads it, laughs, and begins typing a response.*

ZOE: Uh-huh.

PEARL: Zozo, I need to tell you something very important.

ZOE: I'm listening.

PEARL: I wanted to tell you and Mei together, but you need to hear this first.

ZOE: Mm-hm.

PEARL: Zozo, put down your phone. Work or whoever you're talking to can wait.

ZOE: Oh, shit. Shit!

PEARL: What? What happened?

ZOE: Work! I forgot I have a shift tomorrow and I'm training a new barista. I'm the only one with keys because the boss is away. Shit! I'll have to wake up at what? Four o'clock to get there at six …

PEARL: Zoe—

ZOE: See, this is why I needed you to give me more notice about the apartment.

PEARL: Zoe. Right now, you have to listen to me.

ZOE: If I'd had just a week I could have found a place to sublet.

PEARL: Zoe, listen.

ZOE: [*rambling*] Maybe I can crash on a friend's couch for a couple of weeks. Someone might have a spare room—

PEARL: Okay. You hate being here so much, hey? You can't stand living with your Mummy?

ZOE: Mum. It's not that.

PEARL: If you hate it so much, why don't you go live with your dad, huh? Let him spoil you rotten, pay for everything you need. No boundaries, no discipline. Just fun, fun, fun all the time! Your life would be so much easier, wouldn't it? Life would be so easy-breezy without your bitch mother?

ZOE: Mum. Calm down. This isn't about Dad.

PEARL: Mummy is so difficult to be around, you just can't wait until she's out of your life.

ZOE: You're being insane.

PEARL: Yeah, I'm crazy! That is exactly what he wants you to think. So he can turn you both against me.

ZOE: Mum! This has nothing to do with Dad! Stop making everything about Dad. God.

PEARL: Listen to me, Zozo—

ZOE: I have to wake up early.

ZOE exits. PEARL takes a beer out of the fridge and drinks. From a locked drawer she removes a stack of paperwork. She reads it intently and then paces around the room. She moves to an ancestral shrine and lights incense.

PEARL: Ba. Ma. Give me strength to endure what may be coming. I've suffered so much already; I'm tired of being tested. I've been a good woman, a good daughter, a good wife. [*Bitterly*] Twenty-eight days is not enough. Give me strength. Please.

She finishes her prayers and walks to the storage room resolutely. She overhears MEI on the phone. MEI paces to and fro, stopping occasionally to check that no-one is listening.

MEI: [*on her phone*] The king crab is the best dish on the menu and I really want Lana to try it but I know Mum would never let us have it because it's so expensive. Also remember how I told you I couldn't decide between doing English Extension and Ancient History? Well, I'm really glad I chose English because this term we studied the classics and I did *Jane Eyre* and got an 'A' for my oral which means that I'm topping that class, so I'm finally beating Katie in a subject.

PEARL *shuffles about.* MEI *looks around, cautious, before carrying on.*

But the big thing that everyone's talking about is the formal. There's going to be a huge afterparty but I bet Mum won't let me go which is crazy because even Inga the really Christian girl is allowed to go to parties but for some reason I'm not? I haven't even bothered asking Mum even though it's like *the* party and it would just make up for all the other times I've never been allowed to do anything … ever. [*Deflated*] Oh sorry, I'm calling because there's going to be a part near the end of the night where the mums dance with the guys and the dads dance with the girls, and it would be awesome if you came. If you were free? Dad?

Pause.

Yeah, she'll be on the same table as you but you don't have to talk to each other, you can just talk to me!

Pause.

Well, what if you just came for the dinner part?

Beat.

Right now? But I thought you said you were free to talk. Oh, she's calling you from China, is she? No, it's okay. You should talk to your girlfriend. 'Bye, Dad. Dad?

MEI *hangs up.* PEARL *angrily chugs the rest of her beer and then lies down in a booth.* MEI *enters and clocks* PEARL *asleep. She finds a blanket and lays it over her. The moment* MEI *leaves,* PEARL *begins crunching numbers and filling out paperwork.*

END OF ACT ONE

ACT TWO

SCENE ONE

The next morning. Cantonese dance music (a song like 'Love Trap' by Alan Tam) plays in the restaurant/living room. PEARL *is taping up boxes and dancing, hyping herself up for a long day of packing.* MEI *is in the bathroom, shoving toilet paper down her bra and loving the result.* ZOE *is asleep in Mei's room, blocking the music out with her pillow.*

PEARL: Strong woman! I am the strong woman.

MEI *enters, catching* PEARL *off guard.*

MEI: I've never seen the house totally empty before. It looks weird.

PEARL: There's breakfast for you in the microwave. Just heat it up for thirty seconds.

MEI *opens the microwave and peers inside.*

MEI: *Cheung fun!* [Steamed rice rolls!] Yum! Thanks, Mum.

PEARL: You can have the whole thing! It's your favourite.

ZOE *trudges downstairs, looking worse for wear.*

Zozo! You didn't go to work?

ZOE: I'm sick. My boss had to drive back from where she was holidaying to open up. She's pretty pissed at me.

PEARL: Let her be angry; you can't help being sick. Maybe food will help. I made *cheong fun* you can share with Mei. [*Off* MEI*'s look*] Or there's toast, too.

ZOE: I just came down for some water.

PEARL: Sometime today I want to talk to you both together.

ZOE: Okay, later. I'm not technically alive right now.

She exits.

PEARL: [*to* MEI] I think she might be depressed. Or a lesbian.

MEI: *Sik lah.* [Let's eat.] Mum, remember my friends are coming tonight.

PEARL: I know, I know. I already reserved the biggest table.

Pause.

You know, Mei, I was thinking about something. Your formal is coming up very soon.

MEI: I already promised I wouldn't drink.

PEARL: That's because you're a good girl. There are so many people out there who will spoke your drink.

MEI: *Spike*.

PEARL: Older boys who want to take advantage of you when you're unconscious from drinking because you can't say no. In fact, even when you do say no … these rapes happen all the time!

MEI: I'll be back before eleven. Everyone will be at the afterparty by then.

PEARL: Mummy has a surprise for you.

MEI: [*uneasy*] What is it?

PEARL: Something to do with your formal night. [*Off* MEI*'s look*] It's a good surprise. Mummy wants you to have the after formal party at the restaurant.

Long beat. MEI *continues eating her breakfast, unfazed.*

Hello, are you dead with shock?

MEI: Thanks for breakfast. It was really yummy.

PEARL: Hello! Aren't you happy?

MEI: Aren't you joking?

PEARL: Just because you aren't allowed to go to parties doesn't mean you can't have one at your house. I already booked a DJ from the Yellow Pages. We can buy some decorations next week—

MEI: Are you serious?

PEARL: I wanted to reward you for being such a good student. A smart girl. Mummy is so proud of you, you know.

MEI: Oh my God! Mum! Thank you so much. This is crazy! I have to tell Katie.

PEARL: And it's safe because Mummy can supervise! And no need for caterers of course, because that's where Mummy's yummy dumplings come in. Much cheaper.

MEI: [*horrified*] What about just normal food like pies and sausage rolls and chips? We can still buy it ourselves and it will be really cheap.

PEARL: There's no nutrition in that processed junk! Just imagine: karaoke near the bar; Chinese food, buffet style; more lanterns on the ceiling. Do you want me to book a lion dance?

MEI: No! Why can't it just be a normal party? Just music and dancing and finger food.

PEARL: That sounds boring.

MEI: You can be there if you want, but can you just speak English to everyone?

PEARL: What do you mean?

MEI: No Chinglish.

PEARL: What's wrong with my Chinglish?

MEI: It confuses people when you mix languages. They don't find it funny.

PEARL: It's not supposed to be funny. It's my culture. If they're in my house, they will respect my language.

MEI: Fine. I don't care.

PEARL: White people expect everyone to learn *their* language. They think they're so right because … what's the saying? 'You flew here, we grew here.' Hello? Unless you are the Aboriginal people, everyone is a migrant. It's hypothetical!

MEI: *Hypocritical.*

PEARL: It's our house, so we throw our style of party. You don't have to care what all those mini bitches and bastards say.

MEI: I'd rather not have the party at all then.

Pause.

I'm going for a walk.

PEARL: Walking where?

MEI: To the end of the street and back! It's broad daylight!

MEI *exits.* ZOE *enters and sits halfway down the stairs.*

PEARL: How are you? Do you want me to make you some *jook* [congee]?

ZOE: Thanks, Mum.

PEARL: Think long and hard about if you want to have children. Being a parent is a full-time job until you're dead in your grave. Of course I love you both very much, but if I could go back in time maybe I would choose not to be a mother. Sometimes I wonder if I should have waited until I was older, when I knew more who I was. I was a child myself.

ZOE *nods, lost in thought.*

How do you think you'll feel by this afternoon? Zozo?

ZOE: [*snapping out of it*] What?

PEARL: Hello? Mummy asked whether you'll feel better later?

ZOE: Um. Yeah, probably.

PEARL: They need an extra volunteer at Meals on Wheels tonight so I need you to cover me here. It's a different register to the one you've used, but it's still easy-peasy.

ZOE: I've got dinner plans.

PEARL: What dinner plans?

ZOE: I'm meeting a friend.

PEARL: Family comes first.

ZOE: This is what I mean about letting me know about things earlier. I can't read your mind. I've got things on my plate too.

PEARL: What plate?! You're just socialising. Text your friend. They won't mind.

ZOE: I can't cancel this last-minute.

PEARL: [*raising her voice*] Zoe, I need you to do this for me!

ZOE: [*fearful*] Okay, I'll reschedule. Mum … what's wrong?

PEARL: After work, I'd like to see a movie tonight with you and Mei. Afterwards we'll go to the esplanade and get ice cream, talk by the beach. Can you do this?

ZOE *nods.*

If a man with a raspy voice calls, tell him to call my mobile straight away. It's important.

Pause.

It's for the renovations.

ZOE: Mum?

PEARL: Go find Mei. Tell her we can do the formal party her way.

ZOE: [*incredulous*] Really?

PEARL: Just go get her. [*To herself*] Strong woman. Strong woman.

SCENE TWO

That evening in the restaurant. Pearl's done a good job of packing up: most of the restaurant has been sorted into donate, sell and keep boxes. The restaurant is empty besides MEI, KATIE *and* LANA*'s booth. It's obvious that their table was set for many more people—sets of untouched cutlery remain.* KATIE *picks at a plate of fortune cookies on the table.*

MEI: It's really crazy that they all got gastro on the same night. I knew those sandwiches at the tuckshop looked dodgy.

LANA: [*texting and laughing*] What?

MEI: I was saying I hope Nikki and Reese are feeling okay.

KATIE: And Yolanda and Jess.

LANA: Yeah, they're fine.

MEI: It's normally crazy busy. We're just closed because we're renovating. So you guys are special guests.

LANA: It's such a cute place.

MEI: Yeah, it's pretty retro. I told my mum we should keep it like this.

LANA: Really?

MEI: I mean … we should obviously change some things.

KATIE *cracks open a fortune cookie and reads.*

KATIE: [*sagely*] 'Happiness is an inside job.'

MEI: Ooh, that's a good one.

She cracks open a cookie and reads.

'Good news of a long-awaited event will soon arrive.'

KATIE: Oh, your after formal party!

MEI *and* KATIE *wait to hear* LANA*'s fortune.* LANA *doesn't move.* MEI *cracks open a cookie for* LANA *and reads her fortune for her.*

MEI: 'Your present plans are going to succeed.' Nice!

LANA: [*bitterly*] Well, that's total bullshit.

Long beat.

KATIE: So. Are you going anywhere for Christmas holidays, Lana?

LANA: My brother wants to go to New Zealand to visit our mum.

KATIE: Oh! That sounds like so much fun.

LANA: Sure.

KATIE: I love hanging with my mum. Last week she had the day off work so she called school and told them I was sick and we just stayed home and watched Miyazaki films the whole day.

LANA: What's Miyazaki?

KATIE: You haven't seen any Miyazaki!

LANA *shakes her head.*

Studio Ghibli? *Totoro*? *Spirited Away*?

LANA *shakes her head again.*

Okay. Wow. Well, strap yourself in because your world is about to change—

MEI: Lana, have you tried deep-fried ice cream?

LANA: No. Sounds weird. And I'm such a fat wreck, I need to lose about eight kilos before the formal.

KATIE: You are not fat, Lana!

LANA: You're lucky you're basically anorexic, Mei. Asians can eat anything and still look like stick insects.

KATIE: [*appalled*] Whoa. That's really offensive to two separate groups of people.

MEI: No, it's fine. I know a lot of fat Asian people too. Anyway. You should try it!

She waves ZOE *over from where she sits at the register.* ZOE *is texting on her phone and swigging regularly from a huge bottle of water.*

Zoe, can we get some more menus, we're going to have dessert.

ZOE: [*producing menus*] I'll give you guys some time.

LANA: Isn't that your sister? She was in my brother's grade. She was dux.

KATIE: Yeah, she's super smart. [*Off* MEI*'s look*] She is.

LANA: Then why is she working here? No offence, but isn't that sort of pathetic? If I was still here after school I'd off myself.

LANA *goes back to texting.*

MEI: [*defensive*] She's actually a professional violinist. She's only here helping out our mum.

LANA: Reese and Nikki just got a hole in one at minigolf!

KATIE: I thought they were sick.

In the bathroom, ZOE *sits on the toilet. She reaches for a pregnancy test nearby and checks it. Positive. She picks up three other tests and reads those. Also positive.*

ZOE: Okay, okay, okay, okay, okay. It's fine. Bird by bird. Just take it one bird at a time. All the worries are crashing down in waves but then receding calmly back into the ocean. The water's just trickling back. Everything is temporary. Just breathe. No, no, no.

Her phone starts ringing. She answers, remarkably calm, using her telephone voice.

[*On her phone*] Hello, this is Zoe. No, it's not too late. Yes. I actually happen to be sitting down already.

Pause.

Oh my God. Section principal?!

Clocking the pregnancy tests, she gasps.

Oh, no! Happy tears. I'm happy. Thank you so much. I think I'm just in shock. It's such a big step up and I don't know what to say. Okay, sure, I can get the contract back to you this week. Ah. That's an old address. Actually. Just leave the contract there and I'll come sign it in person. Thanks. Yeah, thank you so much for letting me know. No, it's no intrusion. So exciting. Yay!

She hangs up and buries her head in her hands. She notices something in a magazine holder: a plastic rainbow slinky. The sight of it calms her for some reason. She plays with the slinky for a moment. Then she makes a call with shaky hands.

Hey! I'm good, thanks. You're good too?

Pause.

Look, I'm sorry I've cancelled on you so much this week—a lot's been going on.

Pause.

Listen, are you still free? Um. Can you do right now?

She unwraps a new pregnancy test and starts peeing on it.

Meanwhile back in the restaurant ...

LANA: Honestly, I'm happy with a pass. Maths is useless anyway.

KATIE: Oh, Lana, no! Maths affects our everyday lives in innumerable ways—

MEI: We can help you study, Lana!

MEI *looks to* KATIE *for confirmation and* KATIE *shakes her head: 'No!'.* LANA *looks to* KATIE *who smiles hugely and nods.*

KATIE: Mm-hm!

MEI: You should come over one day and we'll cram!

LANA: I mean, I guess it'll give us time to plan your party. Speaking of which, don't let Harrison anywhere near your underwear drawer.

There's a reason they call him the sniffer dog, so make sure you lock your bedroom. Have you thought about catering and stuff?

MEI: Well—

LANA: And you'll need an awesome DJ. I can set you up.

KATIE: Your mum already has a DJ.

MEI: She's only paid the deposit. Thanks, Lana!

MEI *stares at* LANA *wide-eyed, trying to make her eyes bigger.*

LANA: What are you doing with your eyes?

MEI: What do you mean?

LANA: They look huge.

MEI: Thank you!

ZOE *emerges from the bathroom and begins clearing Mei's table.*

ZOE: Sorry, kitchen's just closed.

She slaps a receipt on the table, which MEI *immediately hides.*

MEI: What!

ZOE: Early close tonight. Mum wants to go out and watch a movie.

MEI: That's not for hours.

ZOE: Mei, look what I found. Remember? You used to play with this all the time.

ZOE *produces the rainbow slinky and* MEI *throws it onto the floor.*

MEI: No, I didn't!

ZOE: I've got to go, so if you could finish cleaning up that would be helpful.

MEI: I'm not rostered on tonight.

ZOE: Everything needs to look good for when Mum gets home.

MEI: So do it yourself.

ZOE: Just clean it!

MEI *angrily starts to clear up.*

MEI: Who are you meeting?

ZOE: A friend.

MEI: You don't have any friends on the Coast. Zoe?

ZOE: Drop it, Mei.

MEI: Who is it?

ZOE: It's none of your business. Just clear this up and get ready for the movies tonight. I'll be back in a couple of hours.

MEI: When? What time?

ZOE: In time for the movies.

MEI: Zoe!

ZOE: Call me if you need anything.

ZOE *exits.* LANA *immediately stands and throws her napkin on the table.*

LANA: I told my dad to pick me up at eight. Are you saying I have to wait here for an hour?

KATIE: I can give you a lift home, Lana.

LANA: My bag's under the table, Katie. Do you have pets?

KATIE: Um. Yeah. Why?

LANA: Dogs?

KATIE *nods.*

Don't put my bag in the boot. I bet there's dog hair everywhere.

LANA *leaves without another word.*

MEI: Okay, see you soon. Study sesh! Woohoo!

KATIE *waves goodbye and dashes out after* LANA.

SCENE THREE

Some hours later. ZOE *is in bed with* PAUL *in Mei's bedroom.* ZOE *wears only a bra. She is deep-breathing, on the verge of hyperventilating.* PAUL*'s bare legs stick out from under the sheets.*

PAUL: How's that?

ZOE: Good.

PAUL: You seem a bit … flat.

ZOE: No, it's good!

PAUL: You want me to go faster?

ZOE: Actually, let's swap.

PAUL: Are you sure?

ZOE: Yep. You lie down.

PAUL: Oh, that feels good. Oh my God.

ZOE *gags.*

Zoe? Are you okay?

ZOE *gags again.*

Zoe! I'll get you some water.

ZOE: Don't go downstairs. My sister doesn't know you're here.

PAUL: Sorry, I forgot.

ZOE: Let's keep going. I'm fine. Just my anxiety. When I get really worked up I start to feel nauseous and my mouth dries up … it's nothing to do with your penis.

PAUL: We don't have to do anything.

ZOE: No, I want to. I really do. I mean, I did want to.

PAUL: Let's just take a breather.

Pause.

Sorry—I know you wanted to talk about something as well, but I got caught in the moment—

ZOE: I did too. And yeah, God, this is my little sister's room. I shouldn't be doing this.

She checks the time.

I'm really sorry, but you need to leave now. My mum's coming back any moment. Sorry.

PAUL: It's okay.

They get dressed.

I'm really glad you called; I had such a great time that night. Meeting you, I mean! What happened afterwards was just a nice bonus. I wasn't expecting anything. And that's obviously why there was that awkward moment when I had to run down to the servo. And then the condom coming off—*that's* never happened to me before. I was so embarrassed.

ZOE: Paul …

PAUL: Sorry, I'm going, I'm going.

ZOE: Paul, wait!

PAUL: I'll call you.

ZOE: God, I don't even know where to start.

PAUL: Are you alright?

ZOE: Could you sit down?

PAUL: Are you going to vomit?

ZOE: No.

PAUL: I'm going to get you some water.

ZOE: I'm pregnant.

Long beat.

PAUL: I thought you were on the pill.

ZOE: I was.

PAUL: It's mine, right?

ZOE: Yeah.

PAUL: Why did you just have sex with me?! Why didn't you tell me straight away?

ZOE: I don't know! Things were just going so well that I sort of forgot about telling you, and then I just fell into the moment, and … I really like you. I didn't want this to ruin things—

PAUL: Oh my God.

ZOE: I didn't want to tell you until I was sure. I've taken about a million tests. But don't worry, I'm getting it … terminated.

PAUL: What? No! I haven't even had time to process this yet.

ZOE: I thought that's what you would have wanted. We're strangers, practically.

PAUL: No, no. I don't want that.

ZOE: You want to have a baby? This was a one-night stand situation.

Beat. PAUL *looks wounded.*

PAUL: I don't want you to get an abortion.

ZOE: It's not your choice.

PAUL: So you just got pregnant on your own, did you? It's my baby too.

ZOE: It's not a baby!

PAUL: Fine, fine. An embryo. A bunch of bloody stem cells, whatever you want to call it.

Pause.

I'm sorry. I'm just in shock.

ZOE: It's my body.

PAUL: I know that.

ZOE: Do you? This could fuck up everything for me. I could lose *everything.*

PAUL: Okay, just calm down.

ZOE: My mum would never talk to me again, or oh my God, she would never stop talking to me. How could I let this happen? I was so stupid.

PAUL: It's not your fault.

ZOE: And I've been so sick. I thought it was just my anxiety.

PAUL: When were you thinking of factoring me into the decision? I should get a say in this. We should … I don't know … see how this goes.

ZOE: You mean get married and have a baby together? Be a family?

She laughs.

PAUL: Why is that funny?

ZOE: I'm not a fallen woman. Did you just expect me to shack up with the first guy who got me pregnant and live a sad old life in the suburbs? Maybe pop out another few kids to distract ourselves from how unhappy we both are?

PAUL: I'm not proposing that at all.

ZOE: It's my decision. I don't need you making me feel shittier than I already do about it. I'll let you know when I book the appointment.

PAUL: No! Just wait until we've talked about this properly.

ZOE: I'm booking an appointment. You can come if you want. Or not.

PAUL: You're being fucking selfish.

PAUL *exits and* ZOE *watches him go.* MEI *emerges from the storage room, having heard everything. She turns off the lights and goes to bed. After a while,* PEARL *enters to find the restaurant dark and empty. She flicks on the lights.*

PEARL: Mei? Zozo? Movie time. I bought some snacks from the shops.

No response. She sighs and pours herself a drink, takes an apple from the fridge. She peels it expertly, so the skin is one long spiral, and eats.

SCENE FOUR

Three months earlier. ZOE *is on the first of a series of bad dates. (Note: the bad dates are played by the actors playing Lana and Katie.)* MAN 1 *has a broad Australian accent.*

MAN 1: I've been online for two years now and I'd almost given up. But your bio: 'Single, Asian female'. That really intrigued me. I've spent some time living abroad in Asia myself and—

ZOE: Oh, it's supposed to be a joke.

MAN 1: Pardon me?

ZOE: It's a silly reference to a film. I never know what to say in those bios.

MAN 1: Well, there you go. Beautiful *and* smart.

ZOE: Ha-ha. Thank you.

MAN 1: So what's a girl like you still doing on the market? In my experience, it all comes down to childhood issues. Tiger mothers and stuff, right? Most guys don't get it. They haven't travelled. Not much of a drinker, are you? Neither was my ex. She always got so red in the face. That's common among Asians, isn't it?

> MAN 2 *appears. He's a mellow-sounding, surfer type. He and* MAN 1 *share overlapping dialogue.*

MAN 1 & MAN 2: [*together*] Where are you from again?

ZOE: Well, I was born on the Sunshine Coast.

MAN 1 & MAN 2: [*together*] I mean originally.

> MAN 1 *disappears.*

ZOE: [*bored*] My mother was born in Malaysia but she migrated to Hong Kong as a teenager. My father was born in Guangzhou, and he migrated to Hong Kong as well. They met there and moved to Australia and had my sister and I on the Sunshine Coast.

MAN 2: That's wild, babe. Epic.

ZOE: And how about yourself? Where are you from?

MAN 2: Oh, me? I'm boring. Just Australian through and through.

ZOE: No, I mean, what is your ancestry? English? Scottish? Irish?

MAN 2: Dunno, hey. Mostly Irish?

ZOE: And do you eat a lot of potatoes at home?

MAN 2: You're being clever.

ZOE: If you're going to ask about my ancestry, I'm going to ask about yours.

MAN 2: You're feisty, babe. Bet you've got a tasty Chinese finger trap.

> MAN 3 *has a mature, refined voice.*

ZOE: Yes, it's naturally that straight.

MAN 3: And it's so … dark! And silky.

ZOE: Thank you.

MAN 3: May I touch it?

> ZOE *leans to one side for her head to be stroked.*

Beautiful. Gorgeous.

ZOE: Thank you.

MAN 3: I used to take my children to this restaurant all the time before their mother and I divorced. The eldest, Margaret, is turning thirty this year.

ZOE: Did you know that I'm around the same age as your daughter?

MAN 3: Yes.

ZOE: And you're okay with that?

MAN 3: Yes.

ZOE: I'm sorry. I'm uncomfortable with this. I'm happy to stay until our meals arrive so you don't have to sit here alone—

MAN 3: Women my age don't understand that once you retire that's your second wind. When you're less tied to family and work, there are opportunities for business ventures. Travel. Love.

ZOE: Not for women. There are hideous double standards that mean—

MAN 3: You're one of those young feminists. Well, I have three daughters and they all know that feminism isn't for them because it's a crock of shit. If these feminazis are so oppressed, why don't they do something about it instead of playing the victim? It's a load of hot air.

ZOE: It isn't.

MAN 3: The gender pay gap? The greatest myth after the Loch Ness monster. We're all tiptoeing around these issues because we're terrified of causing offence. But whatever happened to freedom of speech?

Pause.

Besides, have you ever noticed the girls rabbiting on about women's rights are the not-so-pretty ones?

MAN 3 & MAN 4: [*together*] Do you understand?

ZOE *sculls her wine.* MAN 4 *has a youthful energy about him and starts speaking over* MAN 3*, drowning him out.*

MAN 4: It's easy getting your band to headline at a festival if you do it smartly. It's all about social media and …

ZOE: Uh-huh.

MAN 4: Tell me if I'm boring you.

ZOE: No, keep going.

Beat.

MAN 4: Are you from the Sunny Coast?

ZOE: Yeah?

MAN 4: Oh my God. I remember you. Zoe Wong! I played French horn in the symphonic band.

ZOE: I remember!

MAN 4: Do you know Katherine Reeves? She and her husband live on the Coast with their kids. And Donnie? On piano. He and his boyfriend just got engaged. I always thought you'd be the type to settle down. But you haven't.

ZOE: Well, I was with my last partner for years. He wanted to get married and have kids, but there were career things that I wanted that he didn't understand or really respect. It caused a lot of tension.

MAN 4: Oh. But it's a good idea to start sooner than later. 'Cause you know—

MAN 3 & MAN 4: [*together*] You aren't getting any younger. Time's ticking.

> MAN 3 *and* MAN 4 *disappear. We rewind back to* PAUL *and* ZOE*'s first date. (Note:* PAUL *is wearing the shirt* ZOE *wore in the Prologue.)* PAUL *carries glasses of wine.*

PAUL: I forgot to ask if you wanted red or white so I got you one of both. The white's supposed to be very dry and the red is very woody? Fruity? I'm just bullshitting. I don't know anything about wine.

ZOE: Neither do I. I'm more of a beer person, but thanks, Pete.

PAUL: It's Paul …

ZOE: Sorry?

PAUL: My name's Paul.

ZOE: God. I'm sorry. I've just been on so many of these dates now and—

PAUL: Oh?

ZOE: Not *heaps*. I'm not like that. [*Checking herself*] Not that I'm making any value judgments. Women can date however many people they want and it's nobody's bloody business.

> *Awkward beat.*

This is a great place.

PAUL: Yeah, it's one of my favourite bars. Not too quiet, but not crazy either. My sister found it, actually. She knows all the best spots.

ZOE: Oh, you've got a sister. Older? Younger?

PAUL: I've got two. Both older than me.

ZOE: How old …?

PAUL: I'm twenty-six.

ZOE: [*pointing at herself*] Twenty-nine.

Beat. They sip their wine.

PAUL: I've got a brother too. He's much younger, still at school.

ZOE: Big family.

PAUL: Yeah. It's like my parents never tried using condoms.

ZOE: Are they Catholic?

PAUL: No, just migrants.

ZOE: [*laughing*] Me too! Second generation. I think. I always get confused. My parents migrated to Australia and my sister and I were born here …

PAUL: That could mean you're still first generation. If you had kids they'd be second generation. But it's all a grey area because the term 'first generation' refers to both the people who migrated here as well as their children. [*Apologetic*] Sorry. This is boring.

ZOE: No! That's really helpful to know.

PAUL: I'm still learning every day.

ZOE: How long have you been with Legal Aid?

PAUL: About two years now.

ZOE *accidentally drinks from Paul's glass. He watches her, amused.*

That's … my wine.

ZOE: Shit, I'm sorry. Here, you can have mine.

She swaps their glasses.

It's like we've kissed because I've just put my mouth where your mouth was on the glass!

PAUL: And this is only our first glass of wine. I wonder what will happen after our second.

Awkward beat.

Anyway, I guess I've always been drawn to working in immigration. Just seeing what my parents had to go through. They don't speak English so my sisters had to grow up fast and be the adults. We were refugees, but my brother was born here, so there was a lot of bureaucratic bullshit to do with visas that lasted for years. And yeah, even though the stress nearly killed us, I for some reason chose to follow that career path.

ZOE: [*smitten*] I think that's cool. It means that people who are going through that have someone on their side who went through it themselves.

Pause.

Music helps people, but I guess you don't feel as if you're making much difference in a tangible sense. Sometimes I wonder if it's not worth doing. It's hard staying passionate when all you're getting is rejection after rejection and you can barely afford to eat. I can spot a Maggi sale from a mile away.

PAUL: That's the saddest thing I've ever heard.

ZOE: Thanks.

PAUL: I can't talk, though. My parents stuff my freezer full of food even though I can cook. It's embarrassing. I'm a grown man.

ZOE: If my parents lived in Brisbane I'd be at their place for dinner every night. Well, I'd be at my mum's place. We have a restaurant. Like every other Chinese family.

PAUL: We had a restaurant way back in the day. My dad always says food is the great equaliser. Stomachs all speak the same language.

ZOE: My grandfather used to say something similar.

PAUL *smiles at* ZOE *and she looks away, shyly.*

PAUL: You have to keep going with music. I mean, could you imagine yourself doing anything else and being happy?

ZOE: No.

PAUL: It'll pay off.

Beat.

So, are you hungry or—?

ZOE: Quick question.

PAUL: Sorry, what?

ZOE: Sorry, you go. I was just being awkward.

PAUL: Awkward's thc best.

Beat.

ZOE: Do you tend …? Do you, like, think you have a type of woman you …?

PAUL: I've never dated an Asian before.

ZOE: What?

PAUL: You're the first Asian woman I've been on a date with *despite* what my parents want. You're the first woman I've been interested in who's older than me, so I don't have a weird mummy complex. And no, you can't touch my hair.

ZOE *stares at* PAUL *in stunned silence.*

[*Sullen*] Lots of people out there have yellow fever. You need to be on guard.

ZOE: Did you want to have dinner some time? Next week?

PAUL: [*stunned*] I'd love to but I'm working on the Sunshine Coast next week, and then for the next couple of months.

Beat. They're both disappointed.

ZOE: Maybe I should come over now then.

SCENE FIVE

Present day, in Mei's bedroom. MEI *scrutinises herself in a mirror, holding a dressy top against herself.* LANA *sits on Mei's bed, flicking through a magazine.* KATIE *is on the floor, taking notes from an open textbook.*

LANA: You're way too flat-chested for that top.

MEI: Oh. Yeah, I guess it's a little low cut for— *Argh!*

PEARL *has stuck her head through the door,* Shining-*style. She's holding a tray of snacks.*

PEARL: Hello, beautiful young women!

MEI: Mum, don't do that.

PEARL: What?

MEI: You scared us.

PEARL: I'm not scary. It's just your Mummy.

MEI: You didn't knock. The door was closed.

PEARL: But this is my house. I brought you some treats to try. These are rice crackers that are salty *and* sweet. Some aloe vera juice that's nice and refreshing to cool down your brain when it's overheating from studying. And some dried squid for chewing. Do you know that chewing gum helps you de-stress? But I don't have any gum. Just squid.

LANA: Like, calamari?

PEARL: You should try!

KATIE *takes a mouthful of squid.*

KATIE: [*to* LANA] It's got the same texture of gum. But it tastes like sushi. [*Off* LANA*'s look*] It's good.

MEI: Mum. We're not hungry since the last time you came. *Ten minutes ago*.

PEARL: I want to make sure you have everything you need for your study session. You need brainpower!

MEI: We're fine, Mum. Just go do whatever you need to do. Call some painters. Get back to some builders about quotes. Eat something. Clip your toenails.

PEARL: Okay, okay. I'm going.

Pause.

I just got off the phone with your Kau Fu and Kau Mo. They say hello and they can't believe you're all grown-up. The last time they saw you was when you were a toddler and you pissed your pants on the Hong Kong Peak Tram!

MEI: Mum!

PEARL: You were a baby. It's normal to piss your pants. We are all just human beings with the same bodies.

MEI: Mum, we're trying to prep for our exam.

PEARL: Oh, very exciting. Your last ever Maths test!

MEI: Yep. So. We better keep prepping.

PEARL: Okay, Mummy will be downstairs.

PEARL *leaves. Very slowly. As soon as she's gone,* MEI *closes and locks the door.*

MEI: Sorry.

LANA: That was awkward.

KATIE: I love your mum.

MEI: She goes overboard.

KATIE: Well, you're graduating. She's going to be all alone once you move to Brisbane.

LANA: She'll survive. What's Kau Mu and Kau Fu? They sound like dog breeds.

MEI: They're my aunt and uncle in Hong Kong. Mum hasn't spoken to them in years, since they had this huge fight when my Poh Poh—I mean, my grandma—died. She'd had cancer for a long time, so Mum had money put aside for when she'd have to fly over to say goodbye. But then she died really suddenly and when Mum didn't go for the funeral her siblings were yelling over the phone—like so loudly that I could hear it, calling her disrespectful and saying that she should be ashamed. She got really depressed after that.

KATIE: Why didn't she go to the funeral?

MEI: My dad had this emergency business trip and she had to take care of the restaurant. Then my aunt and uncle got really angry and made up all these lies about my dad, so we just cut ties with them.

KATIE: Maybe they patched things up. That's what happened with my dad and my Uncle Rob. They had a really rocky relationship after Uncle Rob accidentally killed some of our geese when we lived on the farm.

MEI: What!

KATIE: He got really drunk and passed out on them.

MEI: What do you mean?

KATIE: He fell on them. They were crushed to death.

MEI: Oh my God!

KATIE: Like, fifteen years passed of them being really cold towards each other, but then one day Uncle Rob made a great home brew and gave two kegs of it to Dad and now they're friends again. Rob comes by for dinner every Sunday night.

MEI: What's happening with my mum and her siblings is a bit different.

KATIE: I was just trying to help.

LANA: Oh my God. Lighten up.

She throws a miniskirt at MEI.

Try this on. You could seriously pick anyone up in that skirt.

MEI: Really?

LANA: Well, *I* could. I lost my virginity in that skirt. [*Off* MEI*'s look*] Mei. I'm kidding.

MEI: Oh.

LANA: It was another skirt.

Beat. LANA *becomes suddenly angry.*

Do you think that's slutty? Is that what you're thinking? Because why the hell are we even friends if you're going to judge me like a little bitch?

MEI: No! Lana!

KATIE: No-one's slut-shaming anyone!

LANA: I can leave right now if you're going to think shit like that.

MEI: Lana! I don't think that at all.

LANA: You don't deserve my help.

KATIE: Please don't kick us in the vagina.

MEI: Katie!

LANA: *God!* I did not kick Kelsey in the vag. She's such a chronic liar. I just shook her up a little bit, not like she didn't deserve it.

MEI: Here, I'm trying it on. It's really nice. Thanks so much, Lana. I owe you one.

LANA: [*calming down*] You're welcome. Yep. Wear that with a crop top and you'll get some cute guys talking to you tonight. You might even get lucky.

MEI: I don't know if I want to get lucky …

LANA: Fine. You'll get your first …

LANA *mimes cunnilingus.*

MEI: Ew.

LANA: Oh my God. Your first …

LANA *mimes fingering.*

MEI: No!

LANA: Seriously, Mei? Your first kiss?

MEI: Thanks, Lana. I'll dry-clean it for you afterwards.

LANA: Don't take it to some random Asian drycleaner. I have one down the road from my house that I trust, so I'll take it myself and send you the bill.

KATIE: [*to* MEI] Did your mum say you could go tonight?

MEI: [*coldly*] I told her we were going to a movie marathon at the Plaza.

KATIE: Mei! I don't want to get in trouble. What if she calls my parents—and you totally know that she will—and then they have to lie to her? And I don't know if they would do that!

MEI: She won't call them! She trusts me.

KATIE: That's why it's bad of you!

MEI: I don't care.

LANA: Ohhh, Mei. Rebel. [*Slow clapping*] Okay, let's just chill out. Katie's about to lose it.

KATIE: I'm just wondering if we can actually get some study done like we said we would because I actually plan on graduating.

MEI *carefully places the clothes* LANA *has lent her in the wardrobe.* LANA *spots something in the wardrobe and sits up.*

LANA: No way. Is that—are you kidding me?
MEI: [*triumphantly*] What?
LANA: I tried that dress on. It cost two grand.
MEI: I got it on sale, so it was a little cheaper.
LANA: Are you wearing it to the formal?
MEI: Yeah.

LANA *smiles sweetly, containing her rage.*

KATIE: I got my formal dress as well.
MEI: You left it last-minute enough.
KATIE: Well, it *arrived* today. I ordered it online ages ago.
MEI: What does it look like?
KATIE: Here.

KATIE *pulls a puffy, lace-trimmed cosplay dress out of her backpack.*

LANA: [*snorting*] What is that?
KATIE: It's a cosplay dress. It's Anna Kushina from 'K Project'.

LANA *falls onto the bed laughing.*

It's a really popular show. People will get it. Remember 'K Project', Mei? We used to watch it all the time!

Pause.

Well, I love it.
MEI: You would, you wannabe Asian.
KATIE: What?
LANA: It looks like something you'd wear to a vampire's funeral!
MEI: Even I wouldn't wear that and I *am* Asian.

KATIE *collects her things.*

Katie? Don't go.
KATIE: Good luck getting a lift tonight, Mei.

KATIE *exits.*

LANA: I can't believe you said that. That Asian line? So genius.

Pause.

Does your mum have any normal snacks downstairs?

MEI: I can go and check.

LANA: My dad's girlfriend drinks this weird soup that makes his apartment stink. She brought back some magic herbs from China for her pregnancy, so if she bleeds out I'll know why.

MEI: Oh my God! Is your dad having a baby?!

LANA: Next year.

MEI: That's so exciting! And the baby's going to be so cute. Eurasians are the best-looking people because—

LANA: It's going to be shit.

A long beat passes between them. MEI *notices Lana's shoes.*

MEI: Do you mind taking off your shoes? Lana?

LANA: What?

MEI: Nothing. And I've been meaning to say: thanks so much for inviting me to your party tonight. I really appreciate it.

LANA: Why are you thanking me?

MEI: Totally. That's such a weird thing to say.

LANA: Remember it's BYO.

MEI: I remember. Can't wait.

SCENE SIX

Downstairs, that night. PEARL *is packing up what remains in the restaurant. She's having a phone conversation with someone interested in buying the restaurant furnishings.*

PEARL: [*on her phone*] Twelve tables all up, and I have some folding chairs that you can have for free if you take the whole dozen. Four decorative fans. One with a tiger. One with a phoenix. One with cherry blossoms. One with a dragon. A television with an extendable arm and portable speakers. What's that? It's LCD. And it's still attached to the wall here. You will have to come remove it at your own expense because I'm too short. A fish tank with a filter. A cash register and safe. One fortune cat. One stereo. Actually—no. No stereo. CDs. Mostly Cantonese pop music. Must go before the end of this week.

She hangs up. She runs a hand along the walls of the restaurant, pausing to acknowledge the dark outlines where photographs and decorations once hung. She wanders over to a stereo and inserts a CD. A song like 'The Moon Represents My Heart' by Teresa Teng plays. She walks around the empty restaurant, unused to the space. Suddenly she clocks something on the floor, beneath a booth table. She picks up a plastic, rainbow slinky and gasps. She fights back tears. She goes to the ancestral shrine and kneels before it.

SCENE SEVEN

Late evening. MEI *is throwing up in the toilet.* ZOE *enters. She pushes the door open to find* MEI *covered in vomit.*

ZOE: Mei? Are you okay?
MEI: [*groaning*] Don't come in.
ZOE: What's wrong?
MEI: I'm fine!
ZOE: You're not fine. What's happened?

MEI *sobs pitifully.*

MEI: I think someone spiked my drink.
ZOE: What did you drink?
MEI: I brought blueberry cruisers. Then Lana gave me a rum and Coke. And two beers after that. Then she made me play that goon game—you know how you tie it to a clothesline? I only had a couple of mouthfuls.
ZOE: Mei, that's a lot even for me. Your drink didn't get spiked. You've just poisoned yourself from binge drinking.
MEI: Am I going to die?
ZOE: No, you're not going to die. That's why you're throwing up. Your body's getting rid of all the bad stuff.
MEI: [*teary*] I'm sorry. For scaring you.
ZOE: Stop it. You didn't scare me. You're just being boozy and emotional.

ZOE *can't stop laughing.*

MEI: What?
ZOE: You're going to be so hungover tomorrow.

MEI: Don't laugh at me.

ZOE: Whose party was it? Was it Lana's? Don't worry. I'm not going to tell Mum.

MEI: Why are you awake?

ZOE: I went to the movies. Then I got an ice cream. Then I went for a walk along the river. By myself. I can't stop thinking of all the cats I'm going to adopt, and how they're going to feast on my corpse when I die alone in this house. Did Katie drop you off? Oh, God. She didn't drink, did she? She was the designated driver?

MEI: Katie didn't go. We had a big fight so we're not really talking. I tried calling Dad to see if he could get me but he didn't answer his phone.

ZOE: Sounds about right.

Pause.

You know I used to talk to Dad every week. I'd call to check in and see how he was going after he and Mum broke up. After a while, I realised that I was always the one calling. He never made the effort.

MEI: He asks about you, though. He cares.

ZOE: Of course he does! In his own way. But he isn't our responsibility.

MEI *lurches suddenly, about to vomit, but instead releases a guttural belch.* ZOE *pats* MEI *on the back.*

Ew! Mei, that stinks!

MEI: It's good they got divorced. Even if afterwards Mum got crazier and even more over-protective and paranoid.

ZOE: Mum's a strange creature. Like, look at this place. What was she thinking?

MEI: I have a theory.

ZOE: Me too. You go first.

MEI: I think she has a second life and she's been transferring all of our food and belongings to her new kids.

ZOE: Ha! No, that's more Dad's style, but you're on the right track. I was thinking she might have a boyfriend? Does she have any dating apps?

MEI: Ew, I don't know. She's being really secretive and won't tell me the code to get into her phone.

ZOE: Yeah, because you used all her data last month.

MEI: For schoolwork! We didn't have any data left after she downloaded that computer virus that told her she'd won a million dollars.

ZOE: Is that when she started emailing that Nigerian prince?

MEI: [*nodding*] And when the scammers asked her for money, Mum got super pissed and started yelling at that Sudanese woman who runs the newsagents.

ZOE: Why would she do that?

MEI: Because she thinks that all African people know each other …

Pause.

Because Mum's racist!

ZOE: Yeah. Mum's the most racist person I know.

They burst into fits of laughter. MEI*'s laughter fizzles out.*

MEI: What if she's selling all of our stuff because she wants to move away and have the life she always wanted before having us?

They both go quiet.

ZOE: No, she wouldn't leave us. She would never leave you like that. [*Surveying the room*] None of this makes any sense.

MEI: I think her plans only make sense to her.

We see Pearl's bedroom, upstairs, for the first time. It's surprisingly small and contains a single mattress, a student desk with a sewing machine on it, an armchair covered in paperwork and laundry, and a mannequin with an altered cheongsam *draped over it.* PEARL *is asleep with her head on the desk.*

END OF ACT TWO

ACT THREE

SCENE ONE

Several days later. The restaurant has been cleared of boxes and most furniture. MEI *sits in a booth with her hair in curlers as* ZOE *does her make-up.* PEARL *is frazzled and can't keep still: first she's setting up a table with food, and then she's putting up streamers and balloons. She settles on dusting every available surface.*

MEI: [*to* ZOE] Can I see in the mirror?
ZOE: Okay, hurry up.

MEI *scrutinises her make-up in a hand mirror and tests different hairstyles.*

MEI: I think I'm going to wear it up.
ZOE: You look like Chinese Ariana Grande.
MEI: You think? What about these side bits?
ZOE: Just hairspray them down.
MEI: And my eye shadow. I don't want to look like Mum.
ZOE: Well, just don't put it all the way up to your eyebrows.

PEARL *tries getting up on the kitchen counter to dust some shelves.*

PEARL: Sticky oil everywhere. Zozo?
MEI: [*to* ZOE] Mum's being crazier than normal.
ZOE: Don't worry, I'll deal with it.
MEI: This lipstick is too dark. I look like a Shanghainese prostitute.
PEARL: Zozo!
ZOE: You're just not used to wearing make-up.

Pause.

Remember to focus on enjoying yourself tonight because it goes really quickly.
PEARL: *Zozo!* Have you double-checked numbers with the food?
ZOE: Yes. Most of it's already cooked and just needs to be heated up. You're freaking out for no reason.

PEARL *clocks* MEI*'s make-up and hair. She fusses over* MEI*'s hair.*

PEARL: What about just down? More good-girl hair, less showing off!

PEARL *resumes dusting, unable to sit still.* ZOE *fixes* MEI*'s hair back to how it was.*

ZOE: Mum, I can do that! Go get ready.

PEARL: What about the bathroom? The mirror needs wiping! And there's a crack on the kitchen counter here that I didn't see …

ZOE: I'll deal with it.

PEARL: Oh! Did you put out the nice handtowels I got from Singapore with the embroidery?

ZOE: Which ones are they again?

PEARL: The ones with the elephants! I told you!

ZOE: I'm kidding. I did it last night. You've only asked me five times.

PEARL: I forgot something. Ah!

She races to the storage room and returns with a vacuum cleaner.

ZOE: I already vacuumed!

PEARL *starts vacuuming.*

Mum!

PEARL *keeps going.*

Mum!

ZOE *unplugs the cleaner.* PEARL *spots something on one of the walls.*

PEARL: Ai ya! What's this big scratch?!

PEARL *rearranges furniture to cover the scratch.*

ZOE: *Mum! Stop!*

PEARL: I have a guest coming!

ZOE: A guest? Can't they come another time?

MEI: It's Dad! He's going to surprise me.

PEARL: [*furious*] No! Your dad is not coming. When has he ever come? He shows up when it's easy for him, when it's convenient for him.

MEI: I'm going to get changed.

PEARL: Wait. I have something for you.

PEARL *presents* MEI *with a large gift box.*

MEI: What is it?

PEARL: A present. From Mummy.

MEI: For what?

PEARL: Just open it. Take it out.

MEI pulls out PEARL's cheongsam *and holds it before her.*

What do you think? Isn't it pretty?

MEI: When would I ever wear it? [*Off PEARL's look*] No, Mum!

PEARL: Think of how beautiful you will look with everyone else in their boring dresses! Mummy stayed up late for weeks changing it until it was the perfect size for you! It's a family heirloom. I wore it on my wedding day during the tea ceremony.

MEI: Why don't you just wait until my wedding day?! If I ever get married!

PEARL: It would mean a lot to Mummy. Poh Poh gave it to me.

MEI: I'll wear it another time! Just not tonight.

PEARL: I might not get to see you wear it another time!

MEI: I already have a dress, Mum.

PEARL: What? Since when?

MEI: I bought it months ago.

She legs it to her room and returns holding a white gown in plastic.

Most of the girls are wearing ones like this.

PEARL: A white dress! Are you going to a funeral? Look at this: so low-cut! People are going to say that I didn't raise you right. That I let you become influenced by Aussie culture. What happened to my baby daughter?

Pause.

Your dad took you to buy this funeral dress. Ha! He says he's so poor, he can't afford child support, but he can afford to spoil you with this shits!

MEI: This isn't about Dad. It's about a fucking dress.

PEARL: Ai ya! Don't swear at your mother.

MEI: I wasn't swearing at you. If you actually understood English you'd know that.

PEARL pinches MEI's ear and tugs down hard.

Ow!

PEARL: Say that again.

MEI: *Ow!*

ZOE: Mum! That's enough!

PEARL: You're so ashamed, eh? You're ashamed of your Mummy, your sister, your family, the food we eat, the way we live, the language we speak. Why are you ashamed, huh? You should be angry. Angry at the people who make you feel ashamed. White people think they're so worldly, that they know best, but then they abuse people and tell us to go back to where we come from. Hello? My children are born in Australia. Where else can they go? It's just take, take, take everything they want from other cultures, and then kick us all out. You're so desperate to be the Aussie girl. But what does Aussie culture have? Nothing but shame for what they do to other people who don't look like them. Dickhead people can hate you, call you names, make you feel scared. Those things only hurt you when you start to think it's true. It's brainwashing. You should be proud to be Chinese! You're my daughter!

MEI: Go away!

PEARL: Mei, are you okay? I'm sorry. I didn't mean to pinch so hard.

> MEI *goes into the storage room and slams the door.* PEARL *paces and* ZOE *watches her, unconsciously gripping her own stomach.*

ZOE: You just pinched her ear. That's it. You didn't hurt her; she just got a shock.

MEI: [*on her phone*] Dad, it's Mei. Can you call me back when you get this message? I need you to come get me and take me to the formal.

ZOE: [*to* PEARL] You're not like him.

> MEI *comes out of the storage room, clutching a day bag and collides with* PEARL. *The curlers have come loose from her hair.*

PEARL: What are you doing?

MEI: I'm going to get ready at Dad's. He'll drive me to the formal.

PEARL: No! One hundred per cent, no!

MEI: He's going to pick me up in half an hour.

PEARL: No, Mei! I don't want him anywhere near my house. I don't want to see his fuck face!

MEI: All you do is bad-mouth him, but he's not the evil guy you always make him out to be.

PEARL: Of course that's what he wants you to believe! You take his side because he spoils you rotten, gives you spending money, pays for all your electronics and junk food. That's not love! That's not good parenting! It's always up to me to make the rules so you and your sister don't go *chi-sin* [crazy] and rebellious. I don't recognise my Mei anymore.

MEI: I'm almost eighteen. I've grown up.

PEARL: Ha! *Grown up!* Eight. Eighteen. Eighty. It doesn't matter! You are always my baby. I'm always your Mummy.

MEI: Act like it then.

PEARL: What?

MEI: Other parents are happy for their kids when they finish school and leave home.

PEARL: Mei. Of course I am happy for you. I'm very proud.

MEI: It feels like we're just living together. Like we're a team, or something.

PEARL: We *are* a team!

MEI: I don't want to be part of a team. I want to be the child! I want you to be the parent!

PEARL: You *are* a child.

MEI: You don't get it! That's why I never say anything in the first place.

ZOE: Mei. Your hair's come undone.

MEI: Go away, Zoe!

PEARL: Talking back to your mother! This is how you repay me for all I've done for you. All I've sacrificed. I carried you for nine months. Gave birth to you. Fed you. Cleaned your stinky bumhole. You owe your life to me.

MEI: No, I don't! You're the one who chose to have me.

PEARL: No, I did not *choose* this. Your father chose it!

ZOE: Mum.

MEI: What?

Pause.

What are you talking about?

PEARL: I never wanted to have a second baby.

ZOE: Mum, don't!

PEARL: I had so many problems when I was pregnant with Zoe my doctor told me I have to tie my tubes straight after she was born. But your father. So desperate for a son. So desperate to carry on the Wong family name.

ZOE: Mum!

PEARL: I was asleep and he came back from mah jong, stinking from his mistress, *one* of his many mistresses, drunk—

MEI: Shut up!

A loud knock on the front door.

PEARL: He forced himself on me. He didn't care whether I will live or die when I'm pregnant, as long as he gets what he wants. Always.

MEI: *Shut up!*

The knocking gets louder.

PEARL: When I was pregnant with you, I found his will in the safe upstairs. I had a huge belly then—nine months pregnant.

Pause.

I wasn't in the will! Can you imagine?

ZOE: Mum! Stop.

The knocking intensifies and then fades.

PEARL: His own wife! His own fucking wife! I'm so disposable! He can just get a new wife any time. I gave him my life. [*To* ZOE] Tell her. Tell your sister how your father mistreated me.

MEI: She's lying. Zoe. She's lying!

Long beat.

[*Off* ZOE*'s look*] Why didn't you tell me if you knew? What's wrong with you? You two! You fucking two. You always gang up on me. You have never told me the truth. Mum, you have never ever loved me as much as Zoe.

MEI *pushes bowls of food off the table. The bowls smash. She pulls streamers off the walls and they float to the ground.*

ZOE: Mei, you're going to hurt yourself!

MEI *kicks the table over.* ZOE *tries restraining her and* MEI *slaps her.*

MEI: You're a bitch. You lied to me.

PEARL: Don't hit people! She's your sister. You're too young to remember, but I depended on Zoe since you were born. Your sister was my rock. She's always been sensible enough to know what's right and wrong.

MEI: Zoe? Zoe's pregnant!

Very long beat. PEARL *is stunned silent.*

PEARL: [*to* ZOE] But you're a virgin!

ZOE: Mum. David and I were together for five years.

PEARL: So you and David have had an affair? Does his wife know? I thought they lived in Canada.

ZOE: They do! It's not David's!

MEI: She had a one-night stand with some random, like a hussy!

ZOE: Are you serious? If we're doing this, then: Mei quit violin and got drunk at Lana's party. It was a miracle she didn't need her stomach pumped.

MEI: Zoe had sex in the house! In my bed!

ZOE: I was already pregnant then!

PEARL: Be quiet.

MEI: [*to* ZOE] You're disgusting.

ZOE: Shut up!

PEARL: *Be quiet!*

MEI: [*to* ZOE] You have to buy me a new bed. It's got that guy's gross dick germs all over it.

PEARL: *Shut the fuck up!* Mei, you're wearing the *cheongsam*. No arguing. Zoe. Sit down. I'm making you herb soup right now. And stay away from watermelon and pineapple for the next nine months—it will give you the miscarriage.

MEI: I'm not wearing that fugly dress. I'd rather not go to the formal at all.

ZOE: I'm getting an abortion.

PEARL*'s phone starts ringing.*

PEARL: Ai ya!

PEARL *exits, frantic. A beat, and then a loud scream from* PEARL. *When she returns, she falls to the ground and bursts into tears.*

ZOE: Mum? Mum? What is it? Did you hurt yourself outside?

Pause.

Are you dizzy? Is it dizziness? I'll go make you some Ribena.

ZOE *pours* PEARL *a drink.* MEI *stands to the side, unsure of what to do with herself.*

PEARL: He left!

ZOE: Here. Sip on some Ribena. Just sip. Mum. You're scaring us. You need to tell us what's going on.

PEARL: It was my last chance.

ZOE: For what?

PEARL: And he just left.

ZOE: Who just left? Who was that guy?

PEARL: I don't know his name. They just sent him.

ZOE: Mum! Who was that person? Just tell us!

PEARL: He was supposed to call me before he was coming.

MEI: I heard knocking on the door.

PEARL: When?

MEI: [*subdued*] Before. When we were fighting …

PEARL: I had an appointment.

ZOE: What kind of appointment?

Pause.

Mum. Are you sick? Do you have cancer? [*Choking up*] Is that why you've been trying to spend more time with us? And the community work … What about the restaurant? Are you really renovating, or are you … [dying?]

PEARL: It's not cancer.

ZOE: Then what is it?

PEARL: I'm not sick.

MEI: You're not?

ZOE: Then who was that person? Mum?

PEARL: Someone from the Immigration Department.

ZOE: [*baffled*] Okay … Immigration. Why?

PEARL: I had an interview booked for today.

ZOE: Are you sponsoring … like an international student or something? Sorry, I'm just confused. Why is Immigration rocking up at our house? Just checking up on the Asian population?

PEARL: Sit down.

ZOE: I don't want to sit down.

PEARL: Both of you, sit down.

ZOE: What the fuck is going on, Mum!

PEARL: I'm being deported.

ZOE: What?

PEARL: I am being deported.

ZOE: What are you talking about?

PEARL: Sit down.

ZOE: I hear what you're saying but it makes no sense. The Immigration people are probably looking for a different person.

PEARL: No, Zoe. They are looking for me.

ZOE: That makes no sense.

PEARL: Even after the divorce he can still fuck up my life.

ZOE: Why would they deport you?

PEARL: Because they can.

ZOE: You haven't done anything wrong.

PEARL: I'm a permanent resident.

ZOE: You still haven't done anything wrong.

PEARL: I haven't.

ZOE: So what the fuck is Immigration doing at our house?

PEARL: Zoe. Calm down. Please.

Pause.

Do you remember when we bought the restaurant? Your father put it in my name. He told me, 'I want my wife to be independent. To have an asset. My wife is the boss!' Looking back, I was so stupid, so in love. I thought, 'I'm so lucky to have a good man who cares for his wife. So rare for a man to be this progressive.' I thought we would prove all my siblings wrong. I loved him. [*To* MEI] There you go, Mummy loved your dad. That was my first mistake. And then I trusted him. Second mistake. He took care of all the books. I didn't know what was happening. I never checked. How do you think your dad pays for all your things? Spoils you? Takes you nice places? He never paid tax. He owes a lot of money.

Long beat.

ZOE: How much?

PEARL: We were lucky we had the Brisbane apartment. Otherwise we would be even deeper in the shits, much deeper in debt. The apartment covered most of it. I tried selling what I could. But I can't work anymore because I'm on the bridging visa.

ZOE: Oh my God, Mum.

PEARL: The good news is that the debt is mostly paid.

MEI: What's the bad news?

ZOE: Dad broke the law, but the restaurant is in Mum's name. And … she's not a citizen.

MEI: But she didn't do anything wrong! It's not her fault!

PEARL: It's not so black and white, Mei.

ZOE: Technically, it's Mum's responsibility.

Pause.

This is fucked.

PEARL: Language.

ZOE: It's fucked, Mum! You've lived here most of your life! You *are* Australian. This is your home.

PEARL: Your father is very cunning, very sneaky. That's why he's the year of the rat.

ZOE: Why didn't you ever become a citizen? Surely in the twenty-odd, almost *thirty* years that you've lived here, you could have sat a stupid test about pavlovas and Don Bradman and a turding meat pie!

PEARL: Hello! I never planned on breaking any laws.

MEI *wraps her arms around* PEARL *and sobs.* PEARL *begins crying too.*

Oh. I'm sorry. I'm sorry I let this happen. You and me. It's always been the two of us together, Mummy and daughter. I tried so hard and it wasn't good enough. I let you down. And now Zoe. Pregnant!

MEI: When do you have to go?

PEARL: In three days.

ZOE: Oh, Mum! All those times you wanted to see us while I've been here.

PEARL: It's okay. It's not your fault. There were things I needed to do too. More community work. More volunteering. Anything to prove that I was indisputable.

MEI: Indispensable?

PEARL: I had to prove that I was *indispensable* to Australia and my family. My lawyers say that if I do those things they will help, it might make my case stronger, or the minister might be more lenient.

ZOE: Christ! There are arseholes just sitting at home watching TV and jerking off who contribute jack shit and they're never asked how they're indispensable to Australia. And then those arseholes vote against any kind of humane migration policy and fuck other arseholes and give birth to even huger, shit-filled arseholes.

PEARL: Zozo, this is too many arseholes.

ZOE: The person who just came. From Immigration. He would have heard us fighting.

Pause.

What's his number? I'm going to call him. Actually, can we write to someone? I saw a similar case where someone started an online petition.

PEARL: Zoe, I get advice from lawyers every day. I've tried so many things to convince the Immigration people. If we call them, it will just make us look worse. Desperate. They don't trust us already. They don't like yellow people.

ZOE: But we *are* desperate! I'll call … my friend. He's an immigration lawyer.

PEARL: Zozo. They will look at my case and go: nobody needs this old Chinese lady who broke the law.

ZOE: But you didn't break the law. Dad did!

PEARL: It doesn't matter! They'll kick me out back to Hong Kong. I've come to peace with that. All I worry about now is you and Mei. It's too little, too late.

ZOE: [*angrily*] It wouldn't be too little, too late if you'd told us earlier!

MEI: Don't yell at Mum!

PEARL: Tomorrow we'll go over everything together. The restaurant. The car.

ZOE: Mum, you're not going to be deported. We're figuring it out tonight.

PEARL: It's Mei's formal night!

MEI: I don't care about the formal.

PEARL: I want you to care about the formal! This is why I came here. So you can have these fun experiences in a good country. [*Choking up*] Anyway, you should be happy, right? You got your wish. You'll finally be free of your crazy mother.

MEI: Don't say that.

PEARL: If you don't laugh, you cry, right? I'm very tired. Leave this. I'll do cleaning in the morning.

PEARL *exits.* MEI *stares at her feet.* ZOE *is already on her phone, calling Paul.*

ZOE: [*on her phone*] Pick up.

MEI *begins cleaning the restaurant: picking up shards of glass and sweeping away food and crumpled streamers.* ZOE *hangs up and starts kicking the kitchen counter over and over. She sits down and starts hyperventilating.* MEI *sits with her and they lean against each other. They sit in silence until* ZOE*'s breathing normalises. After a while, a knock at the door.* ZOE *and* MEI *immediately dash over, expecting the man from Immigration. It's only* KATIE*, decked out in her cosplay formal dress.*

KATIE: Mei, I know we're still fighting, but I just had to tell you that the only reason Lana's being nice to you is to make you look bad. And she told everyone not to come to your party. Because she's a bitch!

MEI: Was my dad outside?

KATIE: No. Are you okay?

MEI: No.

SCENE TWO

Darkness, except for a television displaying the flashing word 'BOARDING'. We hear the soundscape of an airport: chattering, announcements overhead, suitcases rolling. We don't see PEARL, ZOE, *or* MEI. *We only hear their voices.*

PEARL: Okay, one more hug. I'll talk to you soon. With technology it's not so bad.

ZOE: I set your phone up for global roaming so call us anytime and we'll call you with updates too.

PEARL: I know, I know.

ZOE: You'll be home soon, Mum.

PEARL: I love you both very much.

Pause.

I wanted to protect you.

ZOE: Mum, we love you too.

MEI: I feel sick. Like this is one huge nightmare.

PEARL: Mummy will be okay! She can take care of herself. Did I ever tell you the fire ants story?

ZOE: You have to go soon.

PEARL: When I was growing up in Ipoh, I was playing hide and seek with my siblings. There was one very big vase next to the front door. I thought, 'No-one will find me in here'. I climbed in the vase and I could hear all my siblings running around me, looking for me. I thought I was so clever. Then I started feeling a sharp, stinging pain, like my leg is burning. Then my back. Then on my whole body. I jumped out of the vase and I was covered in fire ants. I was so badly stung I could have died. My face was so bumpy with bites I looked like a bitter melon. Your Kau Fu—the Kau Fu I'll see today—he gave me my English name. He said pearls form when something bad gets inside an oyster, and the oyster has to protect itself. It spits and spits at the enemy until the enemy gets drowned, until they can't fight any longer. The end result, even after there is so much pain, is very strong, very beautiful.

ANNOUNCEMENT: This is the final boarding call for Mrs Pearl Wong. Mrs Pearl Wong. Please proceed to your gate. Your flight is boarded and ready for departure.

PEARL: 'Bye, my babies. 'Bye!

We hear the soundscape of a plane ready for departure: the plane door closing, the emergency demonstration, the plane speeding up on the runway, and finally taking off. The television screen flicks to 'DEPARTED'.

SCENE THREE

A blank stage with a spotlight on ZOE. *In this scene, we see a series of testimonials narrated by* ZOE *and* MEI.

ZOE: I've had anxiety since I can remember. When I was eight, my first psychologist asked me to describe a panic attack. I didn't know what a panic attack was then. All I knew was that sometimes, when I let my thoughts stray, I felt suddenly overwhelmed, alien, strange. I called them 'mind attacks'. I'd sit in the panic and feel like I was outside of myself, like nothing could ever make things right. I had mind attacks a lot when I was a kid. Mum didn't understand what they were. I think they scared her too. When they happened, she'd tuck me into bed and sit with me in her oily work clothes for hours until I could breathe again. Until I felt safe.

ZOE *lies with a blanket up to her chin at the end of a crying session.* PEARL *dances soft toys lightly over her face, animating the toys to life.*

PEARL: La, la, la, la. Don't cry, Zozo. We love you. Thank you for taking such good care of us.

She wipes the tears off ZOE*'s cheeks with the soft toy.*

No more crying. Okay, Zozo?

Spotlight on MEI.

MEI: I never thought about being the only Asian kid at school until people started pointing it out to me. Even when I talk I get a lot of looks from people who can't believe an Asian person is speaking with a full, ocker accent. You should see their reactions; it's like they've seen a talking fish.

Pause.

When I started high school I got bullied pretty badly. Before Katie—Katie's my best friend—before she moved to our school I didn't really have friends. I just ate alone in the quadrangle.

Pause.

And even though she was working seven days at the restaurant, Mum came and volunteered at the tuckshop most days. She actually did a really good job of introducing healthier food options, so they have veggie stir-fries and noodle soups now. You should write that down. She never said so, but I know she only came so she could eat lunch with me. And she'd bring me *cheong fun* to eat. That's my favourite.

PEARL *and* MEI *sit together, side by side.* MEI *hangs her head low.* PEARL *pops a takeaway container full of* cheong fun *onto* MEI*'s lap and* MEI *eats slowly.*

She stands up for what's right! Last year, a guy wolf-whistled at me on the street for no reason. I was wearing a school uniform. It was gross. Anyway, Mum made a huge scene.

PEARL: Excuse me! You are a very sick man. You do not speak to girls like that. If you try and rape my daughter I will chop off your dick! Do you understand?! My daughter is still at school too, so you will be locked up for life. Then you will understand how scary rape can be.

MEI: It was the most awesome thing I've ever seen.

ZOE: Oh, Mum loves supporting Australia in the Olympics.

PEARL: [*emotional*] Look, she's carrying an Aboriginal flag with the Aussie flag. I like how she never forgets her roots.

MEI: And she gets super excited watching the Australian Open.

PEARL: Yes, I think I could have sex with Roger Federer.

ZOE: From the time Mei was born, Dad didn't come home most nights. I was never told explicitly where he was, but I had a pretty good idea. He'd just leave the three of us alone. [*Choking up*] Sorry. When Mei got old enough to understand that he was missing she'd get really upset. She'd think that he was in danger somewhere, or that he'd disappeared for good. Mum would buy her ridiculous presents each time Dad disappeared—just things to distract her. She got really attached to this one toy.

Spotlight on PEARL *and a very young* MEI *at the top of the staircase.* PEARL *stretches a rainbow slinky in her hands.*

PEARL: Let's time it this time, see how long it takes to reach the bottom! Daddy would like to play too, but he is busy with business things. Back very soon. But you're always on his mind. That's why Daddy got this slinky for you. To make sure you know he loves you so much.

ZOE: Tell them to think about what they're doing.

MEI: We need her.

PEARL *steadies the slinky, ready to release it.*

PEARL: Okay. *Yat, yi, sam!* [One, two, three!]

END OF ACT THREE

EPILOGUE

Eighteen months later. Afternoon in the restaurant. KATIE *appears and performs a karaoke version of 'Shoop' by Salt-N-Pepa.*

The track pauses after the first verse. Lights up on ZOE *and* PAUL*, sitting at a dining table with beers, rifling through paperwork and signing documents. The space looks starkly different: for one thing, it's no longer a restaurant. The floor has been transformed into a living area—a real home, for the first time.*

PAUL: Probably a stupid question, but have you spoken to your dad lately?

ZOE: Not interested.

Pause.

I'm sorry I yelled at you before. In the car. I was just tired and overwhelmed.

PAUL: It's okay. It's a long process and this is still the first step. Try and pace yourself so you don't burn out.

Pause.

I hope they're not working you too hard.

ZOE: Oh, they are. I'm always rehearsing. Even if I'm not holding a violin, the music's going round and round in my head. But it's good. It's been a nice distraction from all the craziness.

ZOE *finishes signing documents.*

Thanks, Paul.

PAUL *gathers up the paperwork. Beat.*

PAUL: I was thinking, once things settle down a bit, and if you get a night off, we could get dinner. Or coffee. Or something.

ZOE: The abortion clinic didn't count as a second date?

Pause.

That was inappropriate.

KATIE*'s rap continues into the second verse.* MEI *appears in a* cheongsam*, cheering her on.*

As the verse ends, PEARL *enters, cheering along.*

PEARL: See, this is what I wanted! It's so quiet, like somebody died. We should be celebrating, Mummy's home!

PEARL *hangs a 'Welcome home, Mummy' poster that she's obviously made herself. Big, gold Chinese characters are painted on the poster. The words 'SINGLE. ASIAN. FEMALE.' burn brightly overhead in neon lights.*

PAUL: Not yet. Not officially.

ZOE: But she'll be here eventually.

PAUL: It's awful being thrown a dozen different visas. Not to mention it's a bloody waste of time and resources.

PEARL: Zozo, please tell your boyfriend to shut the eff up. I'm here now! Just appreciate Mummy.

ZOE: He's not my boyfriend!

PEARL: [*tipsy*] I want to dedicate the next song to my baby daughter, Mei, for missing her eighteenth birthday. I still cannot believe my baby is eighteen. When she was born it was like something very beautiful coming out of something very toxic, you know? Like a beautiful lotus bloom in a poison swamp.

MEI: Thanks, Mum.

PEARL: Eighteen. I cannot believe it. Sunrise, sunset. Sunrise, sunset. You know, from the musical, *Fiddling on the Roof*?

ZOE: *Fiddler on the Roof.*

PEARL: That's my eldest daughter, Zoe. Come up and join me, Zozo.

ZOE: No!

PEARL: Come on! It's your sister's birthday.

MEI: It's not my birthday, Mum!

PEARL: Mei, Zoe will sing. You must sing too.

MEI: Can't I just watch?

PEARL: What do you mean, just watch? Are you the pervert?

MEI: Oh my God.

PEARL: This is one of my favourite songs, by Teresa Teng. A very famous Taiwanese singer. She died very young of an asthma attack. So tragic.

MEI: Mum. Zoe and I can't sing in Cantonese.

PEARL: Oh yeah, that's my fault. I should have pushed you to go to more Chinese lessons—

ZOE: Let's do this song …

PEARL: No, *this one!* I *love* this song!

She turns the TV on and karaoke lyrics flicker to life. It's 'Chains' by Tina Arena.

I saw Tina Arena live once, you know. Her boobs are in great shape, even after having kids. She should be proud. [*Cupping her breasts*] Not like these ones, you two sucked me dry. And, Mei, I don't know what happened to you. Zoe, shoulders back. The boys like the boobies.

She sings the first four lines of 'Chains'.

[*Talking over the music*] Oh my God, I can *really* relate to this song. Because I was literally in jail once.

MEI: Mum! It wasn't even jail! That's so messed up.

PEARL *sings the remainder of the first verse and chorus.*

PEARL: *Go, Zozo!*

PAUL *whoops from the audience.*

ZOE *sings the second verse and chorus.*

MEI: Oh my God, Zoe. You're going off.

ZOE: Go, Mei!

MEI: No!

ZOE: Go!

MEI *sings the first four lines of the final verse and* PEARL *and* ZOE *join her for the final chorus.*

The song fades out. Lights fade out. The periods in 'SINGLE. ASIAN. FEMALE.' lose their neon. One by one, the words fade out completely.

A song like 'I'm Every Woman' by Chaka Khan plays during the curtain call.

THE END

Belvoir presents a La Boite Theatre Company production

SINGLE ASIAN FEMALE

By **MICHELLE LAW**
Director **CLAIRE CHRISTIAN**

This production of Single Asian Female *opened at Belvoir St Theatre on Saturday 17 February 2018.*

Set & Costume Designer **MOE ASSAAD**
Composer & Sound Designer **WIL HUGHES**
Lighting Designer **KEITH CLARK**
Stage Manager **PETER SUTHERLAND**
Assistant Stage Managers **KEIREN SMITH & KATIE HURST**

With
EMILY BURTON
LUCY HEFFERNAN
PATRICK JHANUR
ALEX LEE
COURTNEY STEWART
HSIAO-LING TANG

Single Asian Female was commissioned by and premiered at La Boite Theatre Company in Brisbane in 2017. The work was developed with the assistance of the Lotus Playwriting Project, an initiative of Playwriting Australia and Contemporary Asian Australian Performance (formerly Performance 4a). The premiere season was supported by Philip Bacon Galleries.

We acknowledge the Gadigal people of the Eora nation who are the traditional custodians of the land on which Belvoir St Theatre is built. We also pay respect to the Elders past and present, and all Aboriginal and Torres Strait Islander peoples.

Alex Lee, Courtney Stewart and Hsiao-Ling Tang

PHOTOGRAPHY Dylan Evans (rehearsal and production photos), Tammy Law (portrait of Michelle Law), and Jess Kearney – Fontaine Photo (portrait of Claire Christian)

DESIGN Alphabet Studio

Michelle Law

WRITER'S NOTE

Michelle Law

Whenever I see theatre in Australia I like to watch the people in the audience. They sigh, laugh and cry with recognition as the story unfolding on stage touches them, connects them, and validates their existence — something I rarely experience and makes me deeply envious. Who knew that being made to feel unwelcome and invisible in my own country was something that also extended to the art I consumed. I would leave shows feeling very alone.

I want *Single Asian Female* to play a small role in changing that for people like me. People of colour. Women. Migrants. Outliers. The Other. This show is a love letter to them. And I want those in positions of privilege to gain some new insights: namely that we are here, we have been listening, and that now it is our turn to speak. But above all, I want audiences to be entertained. These are difficult issues to dissect, but that doesn't mean we can't have a lot of fun unpacking them along the way.

Single Asian Female is full of the things I love: Doraemon, '90s hits, and social politics. It shines a spotlight on labels; those we assign ourselves and others, and how we struggle against the limitations imposed by those labels in order to lead authentic lives. The Wong family women are real to me because they were inspired by people I know: generous, assertive, resilient women who hold the world on their shoulders. And I have been blessed to meet more of these incredible women in the process of making this show.

Collaborating with director Claire Christian has been a pure joy. From day one she knew instinctively how to realise the characters and world I'd created with attention and care. Working with Claire to assemble a team of extremely gifted cast and creatives who gel together so beautifully, like a real family, has been a surreal experience that fills me with gratitude. (Also disgust, because everyone who's worked on this production is offensively attractive.)

This play would not have been possible without them, nor would it have been possible without Lotus, the series of workshops led by Contemporary Asian Australian Performance (CAAP) and Playwriting Australia that fosters Asian Australian playwrights and helped me realise I had a story to tell. *Single Asian Female* also wouldn't exist without the encouragement and support of mentors and cheerleaders like Maxine Mellor, Glyn Roberts and my fellow Lotus Brisbane girls.

Thank you for seeing *Single Asian Female*. Whether you're single, Asian or female, or none of those things, you've made a choice to see work from a new and challenging perspective. It's exciting. It's also exciting that you'll be joining us for karaoke during the show.

It's too late. The doors are already locked.

DIRECTOR'S NOTE

Claire Christian

When people ask me about my experience on *Single Asian Female*, I describe the project as a 'unicorn.' A very special, and one-off experience; a cast and creative team who fell desperately in love with each other, and the work, and a beautifully positive response to the story, and these characters. It feels like the greatest joy ever to get the team back together, to throw a bit more glitter (and neon) onto our unicorn and ride it into Belvoir.

There is no denying that Michelle Law and this play are special. It feels special because it's real. The Golden Phoenix could very well be any suburban Chinese restaurant and the Wong women could reflect any migrant Australian experience. It feels special because it's important. It's important that we tell stories that privilege the other, that reflect the actual Australian society we live in. It's important that we see people of colour on posters and giant billboards, on our screens and especially on our stages, because sadly this is not the reality of the arts sector that we work in and all enjoy. I get to say this from a point of safety as a privileged white woman who has never felt othered because of the colour of my skin, my cultural heritage or ancestry. I say it because I can, because I've been afforded opportunities and a platform and if we don't use our voice to talk about the things that are wrong, well, things will never change. And things have to change.

Single Asian Female gives a voice to the voiceless and talks about race and gender in ways that we often don't. In ways that we should; in honest, vulnerable and angry ways that reflect what's really going on. But, most importantly, this play is special because it's about women, it's written by a woman, and it is masterfully performed by women. Funny women. I know right? Who knew that women could be funny.

It has been an absolute JOY to bring this project back to life with this brilliant team. My hope is that you, our audience, have as much fun and feel as many complex feelings as we have these last few weeks.

Welcome to the Golden Phoenix… you can sing along if you like.

Claire Christian

BIOGRAPHIES

MICHELLE LAW Writer

Michelle is a writer working across film, television, and print. She is the co-author of the comedy book *Sh*t Asian Mothers Say* and has had her writing anthologised in books like *Best Australian Comedy Writing*, *Women of Letters* and *Destroying the Joint.* Some of the places she's written for include *The Sydney Morning Herald*, *Frankie Magazine* and the *Griffith Review.* She has won an Australian Writers' Guild AWGIE award for her screenwriting work, and her films have screened on the ABC, as well as at festivals locally and abroad (St Kilda Film Festival, BAPFF, Flickerfest, LA Shorts Fest, INPUT). Some of the television shows she's worked on include *Get Krack!n*, *The Family Law*, and the upcoming *Homecoming Queens*, a web series that she co-created, co-wrote and stars in that will air on SBS in 2018. She has been a recipient of the Queensland Premier's Young Publishers and Writers Award and has been a runner-up in the Qantas SOYA Written Word category. Michelle graduated with a Bachelor of Creative Industries (majoring in Creative Writing) from the Queensland University of Technology, and has also studied at The Second City in Chicago and the Upright Citizens Brigade Theatre in New York. She is a prolific speaker and has presented at events such as TEDxSouthBank, Sydney Writers Festival and Vivid Festival. *Single Asian Female* is her debut play.

CLAIRE CHRISTIAN Director

Claire is a writer, youth arts facilitator and theatre maker. In 2016 she won the Text Publishing Text Prize for her debut Young Adult Novel *Beautiful Mess*, which was released in August 2017. Her play *Lysa and the Freeborn Dames* will be staged at La Boite in July 2018. In 2013 she was selected as one of the YWCA Queensland's 125 Leading Women. Claire is currently the part-time Youth and Participation Producer at La Boite Theatre Company. Claire was previously the Youth Program coordinator at Queensland Theatre (2013-2014) and the Youth Arts Director at the Empire Theatre in Toowoomba (2011-2013). Claire is a passionate youth arts and community cultural development facilitator who has written, directed, produced and project managed numerous acclaimed projects and productions with adolescents from a variety of different contexts across Australia in the last six years. She was the Lead Artist on Queensland Theatre's Logan Youth Ensemble project TRACTION from 2014-2017. Her plays *Hedonism's Second Album, The Landmine is Me* (both with David Burton) and *Talking to Brick Walls* are available through Playlab. As a playwright Claire has been recognised both nationally and internationally including being shortlisted for the Griffin Theatre Award (2009) and studying at the Royal Court Theatre Young Writers Program (2009). Claire has over seven years' experience in the Education sector, as a high school teacher in both Australia and the United Kingdom. In 2013 she completed an Australia Council for the Arts JUMP Mentorship with Windmill Theatre's Artistic Director Rosemary Myers. She has a Graduate Certificate in Creative Writing (QUT), a Graduate Diploma in Experiential Arts Therapy (MIECAT), and a Bachelor of Education (Griffith University).

Alex Lee and Claire Christian

Hsiao-Ling Tang

Hsiao-Ling Tang

Patrick Jhanur

MOE ASSAAD Set & Costume Designer

Moe is a passionate scenographer and interior architect. He was born in Beirut during the civil war period, which had a lasting impact on his career trajectory. Spending hours on end in underground shelters, the sounds of bombing and shelling ignited his imagination and creativity, with Moe envisioning a reality very different from the one outside the shelter. During his teenage years, he strengthened this creativity by volunteering his scenography ideas and design sketches to various social and cultural institutions during special events while constructing the set himself during exhibitions. Moe graduated with a Bachelor and Master's degree in Interior Architecture from the Lebanese University before pursuing his second Master's degree in Scenography when the program first opened in 2009. He was one of ten graduates representing the first cohort of scenographers in Lebanon. He then moved to the United States where he designed sets for classic and contemporary plays. Some of the productions he worked on for the 2nd Story Theatre and Brown University Theatre Department include *Twelfth Night*, *Amadeus*, *Le Dindon* (*The Dupe*), and *Sons of the Prophet* among others. In August 2015, Moe moved to Australia and started working for La Boite Theatre Company shortly after. In addition to *Single Asian Female*, he has worked as the set designer for *The Village*.

EMILY BURTON Katie

Emily is an actress, theatre-maker, and teaching artist. Her past credits include *Single Asian Female*, *A Midsummer Night's Dream* (La Boite Theatre Company); *The Seagull*, *Oedipus Doesn't Live Here Anymore*, *The Fledglings*, *Riley Valentine and the Occupation of Fort Svalbard* (Queensland Theatre); *A Tribute of Sorts* (Monsters Appear/Queensland Theatre/La Boite Theatre Company); *The Wider Earth* (Queensland Theatre/Dead Puppets Society); and *The Harbinger* (Dead Puppets Society). Since graduating from USQ in 2010, Emily has collaborated on numerous independent theatre projects. She has worked with internationally acclaimed theatre companies, Imaginary Theatre and Grin and Tonic Theatre Troupe. Emily won the Matilda Award for Best Actress in a Leading Role for *A Tribute of Sorts*; and in 2017 she was a recipient of Queensland Theatre Independents Resources Funding to develop a new work. In 2017 Emily once again collaborated with Monsters Appear to co-create the new one-woman show *Elizabeth I* at Wonderland Festival. Emily has worked as a teaching artist across Australia with numerous companies and organisations and is passionate about bringing the arts to regional areas of Australia.

KEITH CLARK Lighting Designer

Keith's lighting design credits include *The Wind in the Willows* (La Boite Theatre Company); *Boy Girl Wall, Packed* (The Escapists); *Handle with Care* (Joymas Creative); *De-Generator, Opposite of Prompt, Angel-Monster, The Machine that Carries the Soul* (Phluxus2 Dance Collective); *Moon Spirit Feasting* (Elision Music Ensemble); *Juice* (The Crash Collective); *Laramie Project* (Forward Movement); *Kazka* (Lehenda Dance Company); and *Tarnished* (La La Palour). His designs for various productions have toured nationally and internationally to Europe and America. Keith is also a member of the award-winning independent theatre group The Escapists.

LUCY HEFFERNAN Lana

Lucy trained at the University of Wollongong, where she studied a Bachelor of Performance. Her theatre credits include *4.48 Psychosis* (Workhouse Theatre Company/Red Line Productions); *Blackrock* (White Box Theatre); *Encounter* (Woodcourt Art Theatre); the premiere production of *MinusOneSister* (Stories Like These/Griffin Independent); *A Midsummer Night's Dream, The Crucible, The Merchant of Venice* (Sport for Jove); *As I Lay Dreaming* (Shopfront Theatre); *The Removalists* (Rock Surfers Theatre Company); and *Machine* (Old 505). Her television credits include *Deadly Women* and *Doctor Doctor*. Lucy is thrilled to be making her Belvoir debut in *Single Asian Female.*

WIL HUGHES Composer & Sound Designer

Wil's credits as a composer, songwriter and sound designer for theatre have ranged from contemporary ballet to musicals, and include *The Dead Devils of Cockle Creek, The Village, Single Asian Female, A Midsummer Night's Dream, The Wind in the Willows* (La Boite Theatre Company); *Elizabeth I* (Monsters Appear/Wonderland Festival); *Rice* (Queensland Theatre); *Sonder* (Queensland Ballet); *Propel* (Expressions Dance Company); *We Will Not Kiss/Touch/Frighten You in the Dark, Caligula* (The Danger Ensemble); *The Theory of Everything* (Brisbane Festival/Metro Arts); *Dust Covered Butterfly* (Metro Arts); *Tiptoe* (Pentimento Productions); *Unnatural Selection, Allan* (Gold Coast Arts Centre/Awkward Productions); *Blak Electric* (Aboriginal Centre of Performing Arts); *Sweet Meniscus* (Anywhere Theatre Festival); and *Legends* (Storyshare International Ltd.). As a freelance theatre professional, he has worked extensively with companies including La Boite Theatre Company, Queensland Ballet, Queensland Theatre and the Queensland Performing Arts Centre. Companies who have utilised Wil's facilities as an audio engineer, music editor and QLab programmer include Global Creatures, Queensland Ballet, Expressions Dance Company, Bay Street Productions, La Boite Theatre Company and more.

PATRICK JHANUR Paul

Patrick is an up-and-coming actor based in Sydney. Born and raised in Brisbane, Patrick is a 2015 graduate from QUT with a Bachelor of Fine Arts (Acting). Prior to studying at QUT, Patrick's TV credits include *Sea Patrol: Season 2* (Channel 9) and *Magic Garden* (Singapore). Patrick's theatre credits include *The Cherry Orchard, Romeo and Juliet, The Man Who Came to Dinner, The Coast of Utopia: Voyage, The Hot L Baltimore* (QUT), and *STEMania* (Echelon Productions). Patrick made his La Boite Theatre Company and professional main stage theatre debut with *Single Asian Female* last year. Patrick will next be seen in the ABC telemovie *Riot* directed by Jeffrey Walker and *Terrestrial* with State Theatre Company South Australia.

ALEX LEE Zoe

Alex is an actor, comedian and television presenter with a background in journalism. She is a writer/presenter on ABC TV's *The Checkout* . Her other television credits include *The Letdown, The Chaser's Election Desk, The Roast, Media Circus, Story Club* and *Cram*. After graduating from the University of Sydney, Alex worked as a journalist, producer and newsreader on ABC News 24, and was a member of the Federal Parliamentary Press Gallery as political reporter for *BuzzFeed Australia*. Alex has written and starred in sketch, stand-up, and improvisation shows in the Sydney and Melbourne International Comedy Festivals, including her solo show *I'm Eating Peanut Butter In The Shower Because I'm Sad And You're Not The Boss Of Me.* She is a member of the Improv Theatre Sydney ensemble, and has performed in Soap Opera, Celebrity Theatresports and the Cranston Cup at Sydney's Enmore Theatre. She has been a regular comedy guest on the Triple J Drive program, and plays Dungeons and Dragons live on stage as the half-orc Philge in the hit comedy podcast *Dragon Friends*. Alex is delighted to reprise her role of Zoe in *Single Asian Female* to mark her Belvoir debut.

Alex Lee

Emily Burton and Courtney Stewart

KEIREN SMITH Assistant Stage Manager

For Belvoir, **Keiren** has been stage manager on *Atlantis* and *La Traviata* and assistant stage manager on *Hir*, *Mark Colvin's Kidney*, *The Drover's Wife*, *Back at the Dojo*, *Mother Courage and Her Children*, *Radiance*, *Nora*, *Brothers Wreck* and *Once in Royal David's City*. She has an Advanced Diploma in Stage Management from WAAPA and a Bachelor of Arts in Communication and Cultural Studies from Curtin University. Keiren was assistant stage manager with The Australian Ballet for three years, touring domestically and internationally including to Japan and New York, working on many repertoire and new ballets such as *Don Quixote*, *Onegin*, *The Merry Widow*, *Madame Butterfly*, *Coppelia*, *The Nutcracker*, *The Silver Rose*, Alexei Ratmansky's *Cinderella*, Stephen Bayne's *Swan Lake* and Graeme Murphy's *Romeo and Juliet*. She has stage managed *I Love You Now* (Darlinghurst Theatre Co) and was assistant stage manager on *Theodora* (Pinchgut Opera); *Hay Fever* (Sydney Theatre Company); *Solomon and Marion* (Melbourne Theatre Company); *The Web*, *Much Ado About Nothing* (Black Swan); and Sydney New Year's Eve – Lord Mayor's Party (City of Sydney).

COURTNEY STEWART Mei

Courtney is a director, actor, dancer and teaching artist. She has worked on a number of productions and developments of new Australian work such as *Single Asian Female* by Michelle Law, *A Ghost in My Suitcase* by Vanessa Bates, *Australian Graffiti* by Disapol Savetsila, *This Witch* by Shari Indriani, *Siti Rubiyah* by Katrina Irawati Graham, and *Barbaric Truth* by Jordan Shea. She has performed for Queensland Theatre, Imaginary Theatre and in South Korea for LATT Children's Theatre Company. Courtney was the assistant performance director for the City of Sydney 2016 Chinese New Year Lunar Lantern Festival. As a dedicated teaching artist, Courtney currently works with Sydney Theatre Company, NIDA and the Museum of Applied Arts and Sciences, specialising in producing and facilitating creative EdTech and special access workshops in the areas of drama, filmmaking, editing, music, coding, virtual and augmented reality, robots for space exploration and physical computing. Courtney is a proud member of MEAA and is the Secretary of the Equity Diversity Committee and a delegate to the National Performer's Committee.

PETER SUTHERLAND Stage Manager

For Belvoir, **Peter** has stage managed *My Name is Jimi*, *Summer of the Seventeenth Doll*, *The Sapphires* and the 10th anniversary production of *Page 8* (with Bangarra Dance Theatre). For La Boite Theatre Company, Peter has stage managed *Blackrock*, *The Village* and *Single Asian Female*. His other credits include *An Octoroon*, *Quartet*, *Oedipus Doesn't Live Here Anymore*, *Black Diggers*, *Venus in Fur*, *Kelly*, *Elizabeth – Almost by Chance a Woman*, *No Man's Land*, *Grimm Tales*, *Betrayal*, *The Crucible*, *The School of Arts*, *The Female of the Species*, *Rabbit Hole*, *The August Moon*, *The Fortunes of Richard Mahony*, *Molly Sweeney*, *Buried Child*, *Dirt*, *Fred*, *Fountains Beyond*, *The Skin of Our Teeth* (Queensland Theatre); *Faustus*, *The Alchemist*, *The Tragedy of Richard III*, *Anatomy Titus Fall of Rome: A Shakespeare Commentary*, *The Tempest*, *Henry V*, *King Lear*, *The Government Inspector*, *Macbeth*, *The Merchant of Venice*, *Romeo and Juliet*, *Measure for Measure*, *The Wars of the Roses*, *Hamlet* (Bell Shakespeare); *Angels in America*, *The Caucasian Chalk Circle*, *Tartuffe*, *Dinner*, *A Streetcar Named Desire*, *The Seagull*, *As You Like It*, *The Sapphires* (Black Swan State Theatre Company); *Blacked Up*, *Stones In His Pockets*, *Barrymore* (Sydney Theatre Company); *Wicked Sisters* (Griffin); *Brief Lives*, *Tom and Clem* (Marion St Theatre); *Dumb Show*, *The Herbal Bed*, *A Little Night Music* (Melbourne Theatre Company); *Eora Crossing*, *Flying Blind* (Legs on the Wall); *The Beggar's Opera* (Sydney Conservatorium of Music); *The Winter's Tale*, *Cosi*, *Diving For Pearls*, *Emma* (Darwin Theatre Company); and *Orpheus in the Underworld* (Queensland Conservatorium of Music). Peter graduated from NIDA with a Bachelor of Dramatic Arts (Technical Production).

HSIAO-LING TANG Pearl

Hsiao-Ling graduated from QUT's BA Drama course in 1997. Her first professional production was *First Asylum* for La Boite Theatre Company in 1998 and she was thrilled to return nearly 20 years later for *Single Asian Female*. Last year she also appeared in *Rice*, a Queensland Theatre and Griffin Theatre co-production, which won the QLD Premier's Drama Award in 2016. Hsiao-Ling's other theatre credits include *Professor Burton's Travelling Federation Show* which toured with the QLD Arts Council, *After China* at Belvoir, and *Shattered Jade* at the Seymour Centre. She has also voiced characters in the upcoming ABC children's cartoon *Bluey*, an ABC radio play and presented numerous corporate videos. In TV Hsiao-Ling has guested on *All Saints*, *H20: Just Add Water* and *Sea Patrol*, and performed in the films *Postcard Bandit* and the US-produced *Tempted* co-starring Virginia Madsen and Jason Mamoa. She has been involved in the development of *Squint Witch* and *White China* through Playlab, David Williamson's *Nearer the Gods* with Queensland Theatre, and *Single Asian Female* via the La Boite HWY series.

Hsiao-Ling Tang and Courtney Stewart

Alex Lee and Patrick Jhanur

LA BOITE THEATRE COMPANY

La Boite is a story of people, passion, purpose and place.

La Boite holds a unique place in the hearts and minds of artists and audiences. For the past nine decades, La Boite has represented the adventurous and alternative. There has always been a strong focus on the development of new work and artists, and today it is no different.

La Boite seeks to represent and engage in beautiful and rich diversity through stories, ideas and voices; the diversity of form, of ideas, ethnicity, gender – of identity.

Theatre has the capacity to embrace difference in so many ways. La Boite pushes the boundaries of form by collaborating with some extraordinary partners to stretch theatrical, visual and musical boundaries, playing with cabaret, puppets, classical text, hip-hop, the theatrical and extraordinary talents. This varied menu enlivens and inspires existing and new audiences to experience the magic of live performance in the unique Roundhouse Theatre.

There are so many ways to engage with La Boite for people of all ages and backgrounds – check out the Participation page on the La Boite website for more details.

Each year La Boite are delighted to share a program of exciting productions that bring together our most talented local and national artists, engage in the discourse around the stories they tell, and encourage audiences to participate.

www.laboite.com.au
#LABOITE2018

@LaBoiteTheatre
/LaBoiteTheatreCompany
@LaBoiteTheatreCo

LA BOITE BOARD

Julian Myers (Chair), Richard Hundt (Treasurer), Vivienne Anthon (Deputy Chair), Graham Bethune, Gina Fairfax, Kevin O'Brien, Lynn Rainbow Reid AM & John Scherer.

LA BOITE STAFF

Artistic Director & CEO Todd MacDonald
General Manager Katherine Hoepper
Creative Producer Sanja Simic
Youth & Participation Producer Claire Christian
Accountant Karen Mitchell FCA
Assistant Accountant Roxane Eden
Development & Philanthropy Manager Jackie Maxwell
Acting Development & Philanthropy Coordinator Steve Pirie
Communications Agency ARUGA
Marketing Coordinator Stephanie Pickett
Graphic Designer Claudia Piggott
Head of Production Canada White
Head Technician Nick Toll
Workshop Coordinator Andrew Mills
Venue Operations Manager Jessica Ralph
Ticketing & Administration Officers Maddie Little & Nathan Mills

BELVOIR STAFF

18 Belvoir Street, Surry Hills NSW 2010
Email mail@belvoir.com.au Web belvoir.com.au
Administration (02) 9698 3344 Facsimile (02) 9319 3165 Box Office (02) 9699 3444

Artistic Director
Eamon Flack
Executive Director
Sue Donnelly
Deputy Executive Director & Senior Producer
Aaron Beach

BELVOIR BOARD
Patricia Akopiantz
Mitchell Butel
Luke Carroll
Sue Donnelly
Tracey Driver
Eamon Flack
Ian Learmonth
Michael Lynch
Sam Meers (Chair)
Peter Wilson

BELVOIR ST THEATRE BOARD
Stuart McCreery
Angela Pearman (Chair)
Sue Rosen
Nick Schlieper
Mark Seymour
Kingsley Slipper
Susan Teasey

ARTISTIC & PROGRAMMING
Artistic Associates
Tom Wright
Dom Mercer
Artistic Administrator
Carly Pickard

EDUCATION
Education Manager
Jane May
Education Coordinator
Sharon Zeeman

ADMINISTRATION
Office Manager
Jessica Vincent

FINANCE & OPERATIONS
Company Accountant
Barbara Lewis
Acting Finance Administrator
Shyleja Paul

MARKETING
Head of Marketing & Customer Service
Amy Goodhew
Marketing Coordinator
Georgia Goode
Communications Coordinator
Cara Nash

BOX OFFICE & CUSTOMER SERVICES
Customer Experience & Ticketing Manager
Andrew Dillon
Ticketing Systems Administrator
Tanya Ginori-Cairns
CRM Manager
Charlotte Bradley
Customer Service Coordinator
Anna Booty
Guest Operations Coordinator
Keila Terencio

FRONT OF HOUSE
Front of House Manager
Scott Pirlo

DEVELOPMENT
Philanthropy Managers
Joanna Maunder &
Liz Tomkinson
Development Coordinator
Kseniia Grishilova

PRODUCTION
Head of Production
Sally Withnell
Technical Manager
Aiden Brennan
Deputy Production Manager
Roxzan Bowes
Senior Technician
Raine Paul
Resident Stage Manager
Luke McGettigan
Acting Staging & Construction Manager
Brett Wilbe
Staging & Construction Assistant
Brydie Ryan
Costume Coordinator
Judy Tanner

BELVOIR BRIEFINGS

Belvoir Briefings are your chance to hear directly from the artists about every show before it hits our stage.

For each production in 2018, the creative team will sit down to talk about why they wanted to tackle the story, how it's evolved in the rehearsal room, and what audiences can expect from the show. It's your ticket backstage.

Of course, there will also be time for you to ask your questions, and we'd love to continue the discussion in the bar afterward.

Belvoir Briefings are FREE but we'd like you to book online at **belvoir.com.au/events/belvoir-briefings** so we can save you a spot.

Sami in Paradise
6.30pm, Thursday 22 March

The Sugar House
6.30pm, Thursday 26 April

Bliss
6.30pm, Thursday 14 June

A Taste of Honey
6.30pm, Thursday 12 July

Calamity Jane
6.30pm, Thursday 9 August

An Enemy of the People
6.30pm, Thursday 27 September

The Dance of Death
6.30pm, Thursday 1 November

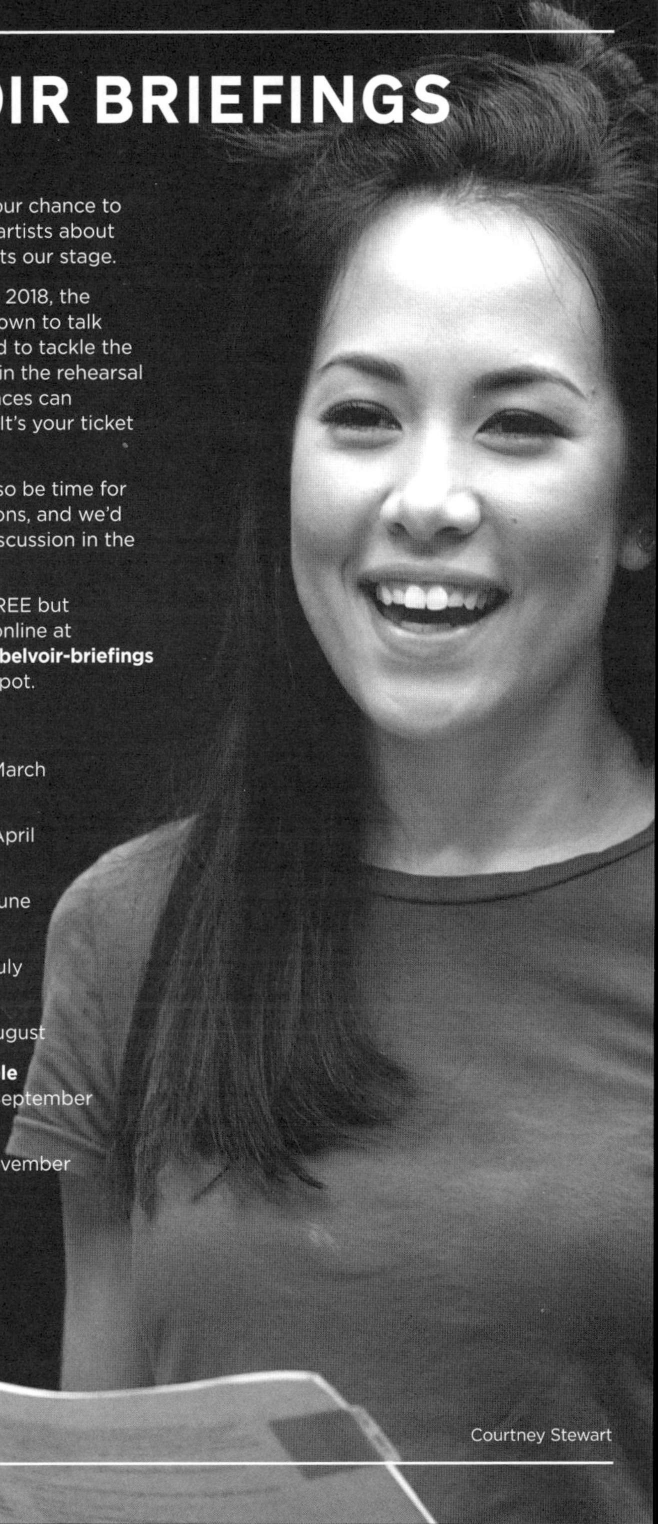

Courtney Stewart

BELVOIR DONORS

We give our heartfelt thanks to all our donors for their loyal and generous support.

CHAIR'S CIRCLE

$10,000+

Patty Akopiantz & Justin Punch
Sophie & Stephen Allen
The Balnaves Foundation
Jessica Block
Catherine & Philip Brenner
Anne Britton
Jillian Broadbent AO
Andrew Cameron AM & Cathy Cameron
David Gonski AC & Associate Professor Orli Wargon OAM
Anita Jacoby
Matthew & Veronica Latham
Ian Learmonth & Julia Pincus
Helen Lynch AM & Helen Bauer
Frank Macindoe
Nelson Meers AO & Carole Meers
Sam Meers & Richard Kuo
Cathie & Paul Oppenheim
Andrew & Andrea Roberts
Sherry-Hogan Foundation
Rob Thomas AM
Mark & Jacqueline Warburton
WeirAnderson Foundation
Kim Williams AM & Catherine Dovey
Peter Wilson & James Emmett
Cathy Yuncken

CREATIVE DEVELOPMENT FUND

$10,000+

Patty Akopiantz & Justin Punch
Stephen Allen
Andrew Cameron AM & Cathy Cameron**
Helen Lynch AM & Helen Bauer**
Frank Macindoe*
Sherry-Hogan Foundation*
Shemara Wikramanayake & Ed Gilmartin
Kim Williams AM & Catherine Dovey

$5,000 – $9,999

Jill & Richard Berry
Anne Britton**
Hartley Cook*
Sue Donnelly
Louise Herron AM & Clark Butler**
Peter & Rosemary Ingle*
Don & Leslie Parsonage
Dan & Jackie Phillips
Doc Ross Family Foundation
Victoria Taylor**

$2,000 – $4,999

Neil Armfield AO**
Justin Butterworth
John Cary
Anne & Michael Coleman*
Victoria Holthouse*
Richard, Heather & Rachel Rasker
Penelope Seidler AM

$500 – $1,999

Robert Crossman
Richard Evans
Ross McLean & Fiona Beith*
Louise & Michael Nettleton
Angela Pearman
Steve & Belinda Rankine
Sally & Jonathan Rourke
Mark Warburton
Penny Ward

B KEEPERS

$5,000+

Robert & Libby Albert**
Ellen Borda*
Constructability Recruitment
Anne Britton**
Marion Heathcote & Brian Burfitt**
Louise Christie**
Bruce Meagher & Greg Waters
Don & Leslie Parsonage*
Jann Skinner

$3,000 – $4,999

Anonymous (1)
Tom Dent
Suzanne & Michael Daniel**
Bob & Chris Ernst**
Firehold Pty.Ltd.**
David & Kathryn Groves*
Judge Joe Harman
Michael Hobbs OAM**
Colleen Kane**
Tony Maxwell & Robyn Godlee
Chantal & Greg Roger**
Andrew & Lesley Rosenberg*
Peter & Jan Shuttleworth*
Merilyn Sleigh & Raoul de Ferranti
Patricia Wong

$2,000 – $2,999

Antoinette Albert**
Claire Armstrong & John Sharpe**
Max Bonnell**
Charlene & Graham Bradley AM
Jillian Broadbent AO**
Chris Brown
Jan Burnswoods*
Jan Chapman AO & Stephen O'Rourke
Wesley Enoch
Danny & Kathleen Gilbert**
Cary & Rob Gillespie
Sophie Guest
Peter Graves**
David Haertsch**
John Head**
Libby Higgin*
Jennifer Ledgar & Bob Lim*
Professor Elizabeth More AM**
Dr David Nguyen**
Timothy & Eva Pascoe**
Richard, Heather & Rachel Rasker*
Michael Rose
David & Emma Scambler
Ann Sherry AO*
Judy Thomson*

$1,000 – $1,999

Anonymous (2)
Mark & Jacqueline Warburton
Allen & Julie Blewitt
Jake Blundell
Dr Catherine Brown-Watt PSM
Mary Jo & Lloyd Capps**
Annabel Crabb & Jeremy Storer
Lisa Hamilton & Rob White
Wendy & Andrew Hamlin**
Avril Jeans**
Kevin & Rosemarie Jeffers-Palmer ***
Corinne & Rob Johnston*
Margaret Johnston
A. le Marchant*
Stephanie Lee*
Atul Lele*
Hilary Linstead**
Louise McBride
Ross McLean & Fiona Beith*
Cajetan Mula (Honorary Member)
K Nomchong SC
Jacqueline & Michael Palmer
Dr Natalie Pelham*
Greeba Pritchard*
Alex Oonagh Redmond**
Richmond Sisters
Colleen Roche
David Round
Jennifer Smith
Chris & Bea Sochan*
Camilla & Andrew Strang
Sue Thomson*
Alese Watson
Paul & Jennifer Winch

THE HIVE

$2,500

Elizabeth Allen & David Langley
Anthony & Elly Baxter
Aaron Beach & Deborah Brown
Nathan & Yael Bennett
Justin Butterworth
Dan & Emma Chesterman
Este Darin-Cooper & Chris Burgess
Joanna Davidson & Julian Leeser
Tracey Driver
Piers Grove
Ruth Higgins & Tamson Pietsch
David Rayment & Mary Nguyen
Hannah Roache & Luke Turner
Chris Smith
The Sky Foundation
Peter Wilson & James Emmett*

HONEY Bs

$1,000+

Margaret Butler
Marla Heller
Tristan Landers
Louise McCoach
Olivia Pascoe
Janet Pennington
Sylvia Preda
Janna Robertson
Arlene Tansey
Lauren Thompson
Cathy Yuncken*

EDUCATION DONORS

$10,000+

Doc Ross Family Foundation
Heather Doig & Rob Koczkar
Kimberly & Angus Holden
Susie Kelly
Ian Learmonth & Julia Pincus*
Rob Thomas AM

$5,000 - $9,999

Patty Akopiantz & Justin Punch
Margaret Butler
Ari and Lisa Droga
Veronica & Matthew Latham
Louise Mitchell & Peter Pether

$2,000 - $4,999

Anonymous (1)
Andrew Cameron AM & Cathy Cameron**
Estate of the late Angelo Comino
Rowena Danziger AM & Ken Coles AM
John B Fairfax AO & Libby Fairfax
Kiera Grant & Mark Tallis
Julie Hannaford*
Judge Joe Harman
Bill Hawker
David Jonas & Desmon Du Plessis
Dan & Jackie Phillips
Public Education Foundation

$500 - $1,999

Anonymous (8)
32 Edward St
Len & Nita Armfield
Nicola Atkinson
AB*
Arrow Commodities
Ian Barnett*
Brand New You
Dr Dee de Bruyn
Jessica Block
Andrew Bullock
John Campbell
Sue Capon
Denise & Robert Dunn
Joanna Elliott & David Ryan
Bob & Chris Ernst
Susan Gabriel
Geoffrey & Patricia Gemmell*
Natasha Goulden
Peter Gray
Dorothy Hoddinott AO**
Sue Hyde*
Peter & Rosemary Ingle*
Catherine Jones
Ruth Layton
Jennifer Ledgar & Bob Lim*
Annabelle Mahar
Christopher Matthies
Mary Miltenyi
Ruth Nicholas
Patricia Novikoff
Nicole Philps
Plaza Films
Polese Family
Richard, Heather & Rachel Rasker
Angela Raymond
Ruth Ritchie
Stephen & Christy Roberts
Geoffrey Rush AC
Julianne Schultz
Peter & Janet Shuttleworth*
Rob Sindel
Chris & Bea Sochan*
Dr Titia Sprague
Cheri Stevenson
Kerry Stubbs
Daniela Torsh
Ali Yeldham & Angus Hudson
Jason Yetton & Jo Lam
Rob Younsman & Veronica Espaliat
Catherine West & Julien Fouter

GENERAL DONORS

$10,000+

Anonymous (1)
Andrew Cameron AM & Cathy Cameron**
Ross Littlewood & Alexandra Curtin*

$2,000 - $4,999

Anonymous (3)
Samantha Acret
Bill Hawker
Brenna Hobson
Raymond McDonald
Ralph Myers
Timothy & Eva Pascoe
Louisa Ward
Lynne Watkins & Nicolas Harding*

$500 - $1,999

Anonymous (9)
Annette Adair
Victor Baskir
Baiba Berzins*
Christine Bishop
Mr Dennis Bluth & Dr Diana Marks
Keith Bradley AM
Ian Breden & Josephine Key*
Anne Britton**
Robert Burns
Cadmium Property
Michael & Colleen Chesterman*
Tim & Bryony Cox*
Jane Diamond*
Jane Mary Eagger
Anton Enus
Gillian Fenton
Sandra Ferman
Tim Gerrard
Verity Goitein
Peter Gray
Priscilla Guest*
Dr Cheryl Hanbury
Jill Hawker
Grania Hickley
Ruth Higgins & Tamson Pietsch
Elaine Hiley
Dorothy Hoddinott AO**
Clyth Hoult
Robert Kidd
Cheryl L

BELVOIR DONORS Continued

GENERAL DONORS

$500 – $1,999 (Continued)

Connie Liu
Elizabeth & Richard Longes
Lisa Manchur
Julianne Maxwell
E.J.R McDonald
Genie Melone
Irene Miller*
Peter Mitchell
Patricia Novikoff*
Judy & Geoff Patterson*
Christina Pender
Susan Pugh
David & Jill Pumphrey
Kim Rosser
Bernard Ryan & Michael Rowe
Leigh Rae Sanderson
Elfriede Sangkuhl
Eileen Slarke & Family**
Chris & Bea Sochan*
Andrea Socratous
Paul Stein
Leslie Stern
Yael Stone
Mike Thompson
Tom Tilley
Helen Trinca
Suzanne & Ross Tzannes AM*
Louise & Steve Verrier
Chris Vik & Chelsea Albert
Sarah Walters*
Louisa Ward
Elizabeth Webby AM
Richard Willis
Brian & Trish Wright
Carolyn Wright

* 5+ years of giving
** 10+ years of giving
*** 15+ years of giving
List correct at time of printing.

Belvoir is very grateful to accept donations of all sizes. Donations over $2 are tax deductible. If you would like to make a donation or would like further information about any of our donor programs please call our Development Team on 02 9698 3344 or email development@belvoir.com.au

SPECIAL THANKS

We would like to acknowledge Cajetan Mula, Len Armfield and Geoffrey Scharer. They will always be remembered for their generosity to Belvoir.

We also thank our Life Members, who have made outstanding contributions to Belvoir over more than thirty years. They have changed the course of the company and are now ingrained in its fabric: Neil Armfield AO, Neil Balnaves AO, Andrew Cameron AM, David Gonski AC, Rachel Healy, Louise Herron AM, Sue Hill, Geoffrey Rush AC, Orli Wargon OAM and Chris Westwood.

These people and foundations supported the redevelopment of Belvoir St Theatre and purchase of our warehouse.

Andrew & Cathy Cameron
(refurbishment of theatre & warehouse)

Russell Crowe
(redevelopment of theatre)

The Gonski Foundation
& Nelson Meers Foundation
(Gonski Meers Foyer)

Andrew & Wendy Hamlin
(Executive Director's office)

Hal Herron
(The Hal Bar)

Geoffrey Rush
(redevelopment of theatre)

Fred Street AM
(Upstairs dressing room)

BELVOIR
2018

AFTT
ACADEMY OF FILM, THEATRE & TELEVISION
A BRAVE NEW WORLD OF
ACTING, FILM &
STAGE MANAGEMENT.
NOW ENROLLING. APPLY NOW.
WWW.AFTT.EDU.AU 02 9281 2400 41 HOLT STREET SURRY HILLS
ABN 87 079 097 920. CRICOS NO. 01544D. RTO PROVIDER NO: 90168.
ACPET
AUSTRALIAN COUNCIL FOR PRIVATE EDUCATION AND TRAINING

How can our performance help yours?
EY's support of the arts helps institutions
to grow, innovate and become more accessible
to our local communities.
ey.com/au/arts
The better the question.
The better the answer.
The better the world works.
EY
Building a better
working world
© 2015 Ernst & Young, Australia. All Rights Reserved. Liability limited by a scheme approved
under Professional Standards Legislation. S1629338. EDNone. APAC No. AU00002474

BELVOIR SUPPORTERS

Our patrons, supporters and friends are right there behind us, backing Belvoir in bringing to life the great old theatrical crafts of acting and storytelling. Thank you.

Learn more about supporting Belvoir at belvoir.com.au/support-belvoir

KEY SUPPORTER

Indigenous theatre at Belvoir supported by The Balnaves Foundation

TRUSTS & FOUNDATIONS

AMP Foundation
Andrew Cameron Family Foundation
Copyright Agency Cultural Foundation
Gandevia Foundation
The Greatorex Foundation
Macquarie Group Foundation
Nelson Meers Foundation
Teen Spirit Charitable Foundation
Thyne Reid Foundation
Walking up The Hill Foundation

BELVOIR PARTNERS

GOVERNMENT PARTNERS

Create NSW
Arts, Screen & Culture

YOUTH & EDUCATION PARTNER

AFTT ACADEMY OF FILM THEATRE & TELEVISION

MAJOR PARTNERS

ASSOCIATE PARTNERS

SUPPORTING PARTNER

MEDIA PARTNERS

EVENT PARTNERS

ARCHIE ROSE
DISTILLING CO.

For more information on partnership opportunities please contact our Development team on 02 9698 3344 or email development@belvoir.com.au

Correct at time of printing.

Also available from Currency Press

Miss Peony
Michelle Law

Lily's grandmother was a beauty queen back in Hong Kong. She doesn't care that times have changed, that Lily lives in a new country and a new century. She sees a granddaughter caught between worlds. So Poh Poh pushes Lily into entering the highly competitive Miss Peony, and no matter how hard Lily tries to wriggle out of it, her grandma won't take no for an answer.

And to make matters worse, she's a ghost.

Glitzy and madcap, *Miss Peony* by award-winning writer Michelle Law is a bold new comedy about our good old need for connection—to family, the past, the future, each other.

ISBN: 9781760628178

Golden Blood

Merlynn Tong

Golden Blood by Merlynn Tong feels like a big-screen thriller, even though it's got a cast of two. Playing out on the neon streets of Singapore, it desperately claws back the extreme wealth it once knew, holding a rusty machete between its teeth.

When her mother dies, a teenage girl is left alone within the four walls of the only thing she's inherited—a decaying penthouse in the heart of Singapore. To make matters worse, she's now in the care of her estranged brother, and he's not exactly up to the gig. For one, he's only a few years older than her. And two, he's a gangster.

Like, an actual one.

Left with next to nothing, the orphaned siblings become a formidable, atypical corporation of two. But it's not long before cracks begin to show. What is the trade-off for desiring excessive levels of luxury? What should be kept in this world, and what should be offered to the next?

ISBN: 9781760629076

FANGIRLS
Yve Blake

Meet Edna: she's 14, she's a misfit, she's kind of a genius and … she's in love. With Harry.

There's just one problem: Harry doesn't actually know that she exists. Because Harry is in the world's biggest boy band, True Connection. But to Edna, that's just a small obstacle.

When True Connection announces a tour stop in Edna's city, she realises that this is her one chance to meet Harry and convince him of their destiny. But how will Edna get Harry's attention? How will she convince him that she's the one? And just how far is she prepared to go in the name of love?

Edna takes her devotion to unforseen heights in this thrilling and hilarious musical comedy about first love, fan culture and the danger of underestimating teenage girls. *FANGIRLS*, by composer, lyricist and playwright Yve Blake, will surprise and shock you. If you think this is just a story about loving a boy band … think again. This is a story about how we ask young women to see themselves, and a celebration of their true, unlimited power.

ISBN: 9781760623425